Anonymous

Facts and Figures about Norfolk, Va

Anonymous

Facts and Figures about Norfolk, Va

ISBN/EAN: 9783744780582

Printed in Europe, USA, Canada, Australia, Japan

Cover: Foto ©Suzi / pixelio.de

More available books at **www.hansebooks.com**

AND

FIGURES

ABOUT

NORFOLK, VA.

Compiled and Issued by the

CHAMBER OF COMMERCE,

1890.

NORFOLK, VA.
GREEN, BURKE & GREGORY, PRINTERS,
1890.

CHAMBER OF COMMERCE,

NORFOLK, VIRGINIA.

BOARD FOR 1890.

OFFICERS.

President,	WILLIAM LAMB
1st Vice-President,	JAMES T. BORUM
2d "	HARRY HODGES
Treasurer,	WASHINGTON TAYLOR
Secretary and Superintendent,	SAMUEL R. BORUM

BOARD OF DIRECTORS.

Jas. H. Watters,	B. P. Loyall,	F. Richardson,	W. W. Tunis,
Geo. W. Taylor,	Barton Myers,	M. L. T. Davis,	R. A. Dobie,
Geo. R. Dunn,	D. Lowenberg,	V. D. Groner,	L. D. Smith,
N. M. Osborne,	W. M. Hannah,	A. P. Thom,	

CHAMBER OF COMMERCE,

NORFOLK, VA., October 28, 1890.

At a quarterly meeting of this body, held in their rooms this day, the following report was offered by the Secretary concerning the trade and commerce of this port, together with such other facts and figures relating to our growth in population, real estate values, etc., that by the unanimous vote of the large membership present, it was ordered that *ten thousand copies* of it be printed in pamphlet form for general circulation. After the transaction of other business, and partaking of an acceptable lunch, which is usual on these occasions, the meeting adjourned.

SAMUEL R. BORUM,
Sec'y and Supt.

WILLIAM LAMB,
President.

SECRETARY'S REPORT.

INTRODUCTION.

To the President and Members of the Chamber of Commerce:

GENTLEMEN—The conspicuous position which the city of Norfolk holds to-day in the hearts of her own people, and in the minds of the outside world by reason of her grand location and climate, her splendid harbor, and deep water, is too plainly seen to be disputed, and while we rejoice at the marked evidences of advancement which have already been made, we should not pause in our efforts to encourage and promote its increase.

This Chamber in its steady efforts to make public the growing trade and commerce of our city, in collecting and publishing the statistics of this port, as well as its forward movements in real estate values, and industrial development, deserves notable mention.

So plain is this fact, that letters of enquiry are almost daily received at this Chamber from writers in various parts of the country, asking for the fullest information upon matters of transportation, land values and sites for manufacturing, water courses, soil, health, climate, etc., as may be desirable to those looking for a new home, or for the investment of capital.

With this demand upon us, I have concluded to submit to this meeting a report designed to cover the information which is being sought, and which, if it shall meet your approval, may be put in convenient shape for circulation.

To "strike while the iron is hot" is a maxim which should govern us to-day.

Respectfully submitted,

SAMUEL R. BORUM,
Sec'y and Supt.

TO THE READER.

This pamphlet is issued for the sole purpose of making you acquainted with Norfolk's advancement in trade, commerce, and industrial growth.

To make this more striking, comparison is made with former years, before we could boast of *nine* railroads, and twice as many steamship lines terminating in this harbor.

In location and situation, the city of NORFOLK needs no introduction at our hands; every map published within the two past centuries, contains the information that it is situated in Eastern Virginia, on the Elizabeth river, *seventeen* miles from the Atlantic ocean by land, and about *thirty* miles by water through the Chesapeake bay and Hampton Roads, whose waters are broad enough, and deep enough to float the largest ships in the world. Other pages of this work will tell of its great harbor, and limitless facilities for trade and commerce with all portions of the wide world, and of its internal and natural advantages as a home, or for the profitable employment of capital.

In mercantile pursuits our city is well represented in all the leading lines of trade. The grocery and provision interests being the largest, maintains eighteen wholesale houses, with an aggregate business of $5,000,000—with an additional 240 retail establishments, aggregating probably as much more.

The hay, grain and feed business has grown to large proportions, and is represented by several firms who supply in car-load lots, and at retail, the several articles in that line. The aggregate trade is estimated at $1,000,000, and elsewhere will be found in our statistics, the comparitive receipts from January 1, 1888, to the date of this publication.

In hardware, boots and shoes, dry goods, hats, drugs, clothing, jewelry, bakers and confectionery, notions, millinery and fancy goods, books and stationery, paper, wood and willow ware, furniture, carpets, and household furnishings, we have good representation, and in qualities and styles to please a cultured, refined and exacting taste.

In the line of household supplies we name coal, ice, wood, stoves, tinware, and in fact in all needful articles, an ample supply for every demand.

In agricultural implements and machinery, carriage, wagon and harness, we have several large establishments manufacturing their stock to meet a trade, estimated at $2,000,000.

Several foundries and machine shops doing a large business, and five large establishments for furnishing of supplies to factories, railroads and steamboats, builders and millers, and the business is a large and profitable one.

Ten fertilizing establishments working large forces, and several dealers besides, supply every demand from our farmers and truckers, and the business is constantly growing.

In our harbor we have a well-equipped establishment for the preparation of logs, piles and lumber by the most advanced creosoting process known at this time. Its business, which began four years ago, has now spread over many states, and its work has proved not only satisfactory to leading engineers, but saved many thousands of dollars from the certain destruction by the worm which attacks with marked fury the uncreosoted pile, or log. The material for wharf building, docks, railroad ties, etc., which this establishment is now putting out, places it in the front with other leading and profitable industries.

But it is not altogether in the line of mercantile pursuits and manufacturing industries that we crave for Norfolk your notice and admiration.

It is in her natural resources, and the boundless limit to which these may be cultivated and multiplied, that gives her marked distinction in comparison with any other place, or city, on the Atlantic seaboard.

As a mart, she is conspicuous in *lumber, coal, oysters, early vegetables, peanuts and cotton*, and these by the forces now employed, may be almost indefinitely multiplied.

Within the past decade these opportunities have attracted the attention of capitalists, and transportation managers, until one after another, following in quick succession, have given the port direct and speedy access to the cotton centres of the south, and to the granaries and provision depots in the west. Here they may pour their millions of tonnage, and find every facility for its quick shipment through this harbor unobstructed at all seasons to the leading markets of the world.

OUR LUMBER TRADE.

There is no article of Southern production that can vie with lumber in its importance to this port Prior to the year 1860 the manufacture of lumber in this section, was a financial disaster to every one who engaged in it.

Not that we lacked the crude material, in the millions of acres near at hand, of Southern pine, oak, ash, poplar, maple, chestnut, gum and other woods; but the machinery, skilled labor and direction, with a limited market for the manufactured product. Since about 1870 a new and prosperous era has favored that trade.

In that year the total production of manufactured lumber, ready for the hand of the carpenter to mould into use, was given at fifty millions of feet; and now, in 1890, it reaches the stupendous figure of three hundred and twenty millions of feet, cut from the forest, sawed and dressed by the most approved machinery, some of which is original with our local millers, patented and controlled by them, and not in use by any other lumber manufacturers in this country.

The capital invested in this branch of trade and industry, in order to produce such an immense output of lumber, is greater by many times than any other branch of business in this locality.

There is no article of our commerce that gives employment to so many persons, or that maintains so many families by the large amounts of money annually paid out to a class of laborers and mechanics as is distributed by our producers of manufactured lumber.

To make these facts plainer, we give the figures in detail as furnished the Chamber of Commerce by the Lumbermen's Committee.

" There are in and around Norfolk sixty (60) saw mills and planing mills whose annual production is now three hundred and twenty million (320,000,000) feet of lumber, worth about 4,500,000 dollars at wholesale prices.

These mills employ about (5,000) five thousand men; their pay-rolls aggregate ($150,000) one hundred and fifty thousand dollars per month, or nearly ($2,000,000) two millions of dollars annually.

In addition to these figures, these mills require thousands of dollars worth of provisions for their men, and many more thousands of dollars worth of hay and feed for the great number of cattle employed in hauling timber and logs out of the forest.

This, together with a large amount paid out for chains, axes, rope and other supplies needed in this work,' places the lumber interest, in this immediate locality, very far ahead in the line of *home* profit and production of any other branch of business enterprises in our midst ; and it is growing larger and larger every year in order to supply the increasing demand from all parts of this great country, for Southern pine lumber.

Norfolk, therefore, becomes the distributing point for this large output of lumber, and, at times, it is almost impossible to secure ready transportation for it, even with our numerous lines of railroad and steamers ; but when the fact is stated that three hundred and twenty millions feet requires 32,000 freight cars of 10,000 feet each, or 3,200 vessels of 200 tons each, to carry this lumber away, some idea may be formed as to the requirements for transportation facilities, and occasional delays made obvious.

The amount of capital invested in these mills and outstanding timber exceeds ($5,000,000) five millions of dollars.

Our trade in staves, shingles, railroad ties and other prepared lumber, for coastwise and foreign demand, is estimated at not less than ($1,500,000) one million five hundred thousand dollars.

COAL.

In addition to our local trade in coal for home consumption, which is estimated at 55,000 tons, we have at our doors the great depot at Lambert's Point, where the celebrated Pocahontas mines deposit their product for sale and delivery, and which is now conceded to be the best steam coal produced in this country from any source. The pier constructed at this point was constructed in 1884. It is 894 feet long and 60 feet wide, with an extreme height of 48 feet above high water mark. The water is twenty-six feet deep at low tide, where the largest class of vessels can take on cargoes of this famous steam coal. The loading is done to expedite the demand both day and night.

From this pier at Lambert's Point there was delivered by the agents

in 1886	504,153 tons
in 1887	695,822 "
in 1888	883,759 "
in 1889	1,020,508 "
Giving a total of	3,104,242 tons

for the four years named, and which was delivered to 3,821 steamers, brigs, ships and other sailing craft, both large and small.

It may be added that the Norfolk & Western Railroad Co., the owners of these now celebrated mines have, within the present year, doubled their capacity for storage at Lambert's Point, that they may be fully prepared to supply the demand which is steadily growing.

Their stately piers in our harbor, only two miles below the city, do not fail to attract the attention of every person who reaches our city through the broad and deep waters of the Elizabeth.

OUR OYSTER TRADE.

The waters of the Chesapeake Bay and the rivers and creeks by which they are washed are known the world over for the immense beds of oysters which lie beneath their surface, and many thousands of men, both white and colored, earn their living at "oystering."

For the shucking and preparing these oysters for other markets, there are about twenty firms engaged in this business in Norfolk and its suburbs. The total "catch" for a season will average about 2,000,000 bushels. The season lasts about eight months, say from September 1st to April 30th, and boats carrying from ten bushels to hundreds of bushels are constantly employed to supply the demand for this and other cities.

This industry enables a large portion of our population to live comfortably, and they like the work.

In 1878 the estimate made of our oyster trade was $350,000, and in 1886 has grown to the surprising amount of $2,500,000 per annum.

Our state authorities reported in the last year named that there were 18,864 persons engaged in fisheries, all of which are in tidewater Virginia. Norfolk, being the center of this great business, the report gives the capital employed at $1,914,119, and the value of the products at $3,124,444.

TRUCK, OR EARLY VEGETABLES.

Norfolk may be said to be the centre of the greatest market garden in the United States. These great truck farms extend over an area of about twenty-five miles in diameter, covering Norfolk county and a part of Princess Anne and Nansemond, and no other section of like proportions can show the amount of truck produced by this or the amount of cash received for the produce.

The heart of the trucking season lasts about six weeks, covering June and a part of May and July. During this period our large transportation lines put on extra steamships, and a daily line is established between Norfolk and all of the Northern markets. From the best information obtainable, we would estimate that the movement of truck during these six weeks average between 250,000 and 300,000 packages per week, or about 1,700,000 packages during the season. To handle this immense volume of produce, both in gathering and preparing for market and in its transportation, a very large number of people are required, a large proportion of whom have to be drawn from other parts of the country, principally North Carolina, though many come from long distances during the season.

This trade in 1879 was estimated by growers and dealers at $1,751,645, and for the current year it is estimated to have reached about $4,500,000, as the following schedule will justify :

KIND		QUANTITY.	VALUE.
Cabbage,	barrels	347,130	$ 433,912 50
Potatoes,	"	500,000	1,500,000 00
Spinach,	"	122,829	245,658 00
Kale,	"	177,707	177,707 00
Lettuce,	"	8,174	28,609 00
Melons,	"	836,152	104,519 00
Tomatoes,	boxes	92,591	69,443 25
Beans,	"	80,935	121,462 50
Cucumbers,	"	46,280	34,710 00
Peas	"	185,415	324,476 25
Asparagus	"	2,928	17,568 00
Berries,	quarts	9,465,306	946,539 60
Misc. vegetables, pckgs.		180,949	536,241 75
Total			4,541,077 85

OUR PEANUT TRADE.

Virginia is recognized as the largest producer of peanuts. North Carolina and Tennessee also produce them, but statistics show that they fall far behind our own state, and, in fact, the crop of these two states combined in the fifteen years from 1874 to 1888 inclusive, did not equal Virginia's production by about seven and a half millions of bushels. The crop in Virginia in 1874 was estimated at 225,000 bushels, and in 1888 at 2,250,000 bushels. Last year (1889) the crop was very short, owing to unseasonable weather, but the crop for the present year, 1890, (now coming into market) is estimated at 2,700,000 bushels of good quality, and exceeds the crop of 1889 by 1,100,000 bushels. It will therefore be seen that this year's crop is likely to turn into the pockets of our farmers about two million of dollars ($2,000,000) as the proceeds of that crop, and Norfolk merchants will handle, as usual, a liberal share of this crop.

PEANUT FACTORIES.

There are four large buildings in this city devoted to the purpose of cleaning and grading peanuts. These establishments are operated by different companies, who employ a large number of operatives, a majority of whom are colored women and girls. The nuts are taken from the farmer and put through machines which take off the dirt and polish the shell. This machine is a Norfolk invention, and the process is a secret one. There is also a bleaching process, a Norfolk invention, which is applied to mildewed nuts to brighten them, thus materially enhancing their market value. ♥

The amount of capital required in the business is between $400,000 and $500,000, working between 600 and 800 operatives, male and female, earning quite $75,000 per annum wages in the re-cleaning and hand-picking process.

This city has for years occupied a leading position among the few large peanut markets of the world.

OUR COTTON TRADE.

Until about the year 1858 the receipts of cotton at this port were almost too insignificent to be noticed in our trade reports. The section of country then trading in Norfolk produced largely of corn, oats and peas, and these were the principle articles at that time to which the farmer gave his attention. But about this period the attention of these farmers was turned to the cultivation of the great staple as being more certain and profitable to them.

The following table exhibits the receipts of cotton by bales at Norfolk for the years named, beginning with September 1st and ending with August 31st of each year :

Year.	Bales.	Year.	Bales.
1858-'9	6,174	1876-'7	509,612
1859-'60	17,777	1877-'8	430,557
1860-'1	33,193	1878 '9	443,285
[1861 to 1865—the Civil war.]		1879-'80	597,086
1865-'6	59,086	1880-'1	713,026
1866-'7	126,287	1881-'2	622,883
1867-'8	155,591	1982-'3	800,133
1868-'9	164,789	1883-'4	582,837
1869-'70	178,352	1884-'5	548,823
1870-'1	302,930	1885 '6	562,580
1871-'2	258,730	1886-'7	556,538
1872-'3	465,412	1887-'8	500,308
1873 '4	472,446	1888-'9	506,171
1874-'5	393,672	1889-'90	412,741
1875-'6	469,998		

And for the present crop of 1890 the receipts from September 1st to December 13th were 342,795 bales, being an excess of 86,059 bales compared with a like period in 1889.

The falling off in our receipts since 1883 was attributable to reduced crops in the Carolinas, and the combination of transportation companies in diverting the staple to West Point, in this State, which otherwise would have been brought to this port. The tide, however, is already turning in our favor, as shown in the receipts of the present season at both places; the figures being furnished by our Cotton Exchange as follows :

WEST POINT, VA.

Receipts from Sept. 1, 1889, to December 13........200,006 bales
 "   for same period this year....... 191,299   "

                                                    ————
Decrease....   8,707   "

NORFOLK, VA.

Receipts from Sept. 1, 1890, to Dec. 13.......... .. 342,795 bales
"   for same period last year..... ....256,736 "

Increase...... .... 86,059 "

The recent completion of the Norfolk & Carolina Railroad and the Atlantic & Danville has contributed largely to our trade this year in cotton and general merchandise as well; and upon the extension of the Seaboard & Roanoke system to Atlanta, Ga., which will be completed before the next cotton season—these lines will greatly augment our receipts.

Norfolk has now five powerful presses with capacity for compressing 7,000 bales in twenty-four hours, or 4.000 bales in twelve hours of day labor, and it may be claimed that with low rates of handling and port charges, Norfolk has no rival upon the Atlantic coast for the handling of this great southern product.

OUR EXPORT TRADE.

We obtain from the Collector of Customs at this port the following figures, giving tonnage and values at this port for the fiscal years ending June 30th, from 1870 to 1890 inclusive:

Year	Tonnage	Value	Year	Tonnage	Value
1870.....	13,502	$ 886,594	1881....	127,964	$16,264,137
1871......	19,174	727,997	1882......	120,838	19,845,337
1872......	20,371	975,793	1883	99,282	14,315,298
1873.....	30,795	1,255,420	1884......	103,014	15,585,377
1874.....	48,675	3,701,006	1885......	85,261	10,341,709
1875.....	53,638	6,395,162	1886.....	185,150	14,145,211
1876....	66,138	7,815,112	1887....	259,814	14,714,404
1877......	62,148	6,277,249	1888......	259,291	13,812,641
1878.....	84,771	10,029,248	1889......	335,021	12,813,854
1879......	108,287	9,820,258	1890.....	401,217	14,247,477
1880......	132,608	18,166,959			

Variations in these figures for the several years is accounted for in our cotton receipts, which is the leading article in our export trade.

Other merchandise and products consist of coal, lumber, timber, staves, bark, corn, wheat, flour, naval stores, cattle, tobacco and other miscellaneous articles of minor note.

Vessel entered and cleared at this port during the fiscal year ending June 30th, 1890 :

DIRECTION	ENTERED		CLEARED	
	No.	Tons	No.	Tons
Foreign..........................	107	111,460	353	416,149
Coastwise........................	1,350	1,371,315	1,154	1,115,771
Total.....................	1,457	1,482,775	1,507	1,531,920

From U. S. Treasury Department, Statistical Bureau, November report, we find the exports for three Virginia ports, as follows :

	For 10 months ending Oct. 31, 1890.	For 10 months ending Oct. 31, 1889.
Norfolk	$10,486,106	$7,003,306
Newport News.....................	6,537,690	5,085,368
Richmond.................	4,372,064	7,061,884

Increase in 1890, Norfolk...............49 75 per cent.			
"	"	Newport News.........28.00	"
Decrease	"	Richmond.... ....38.00	"

NORFOLK'S ANNUAL BUSINESS.

In 1880 the aggregate of our total trade was placed at $38,200,436. It 1883 it was estimated to be £55,011.656. Whether these figures were approximated with sound judgment or not, it is not our task now to question them ; but with better facilities employed at this Chamber for the past three years, we can furnish figures more nearly approximating accuracy than has heretofore been possible.

By diligent efforts we can now obtain statistical information from transportation companies which, in the years above named, was almost impossible, and steady application to this work will soon enable us to defy criticism.

From our schedule we compile the following figures as showing in part, our receipts for the year 1889 :

Groceries and Provisions.

Flour, barrels.............	221,400	Butter, pounds......... ...	1,004,050
Pork, "	13,600	Lard, "	3,274,550
Fish, "	27,000	Cheese, "	709,200
Sugar "	28,565	Meat, " 19,791,920
Molasses and Syrups, bbls.,	6,588	Coffee, "	1,160,520
Beef (salt), bbls.......... ..	1,100	Tea, packages.............	2,060

Hay and Grain Products.		Miscellaneous.	
		Cotton Seed Oil, bbls	29,970
		Naval Stores, "	22,375
Hay, tons	12,648	Cattle, head	7,343
Corn, bushels	819,401	Hogs and Sheep, head	6,811
Oats, bushels	272,397	Coal Oil, barrels	41,000
Cornmeal, bushels	239,995	Eggs, packages	31,219
Rice, "	19,370	Pig Iron, tons	89,265
Bran, "	153,158	Pocahontas Coal, tons	1,020,508
Rye, "	6,248	Tobacco, hogsheads	21,003
		" packages	116,806

This report precludes at this date the receipts for the year 1890, which now show, by comparison for the expired months, large gains in all leading articles over the year 1889.

We find in Norfolk more than 1,380 tradesmen, artisans, professions and other of miscellaneous avocations which aggregate a large business. Figures, therefore, computed with care, give us the total of about $75,000,000 of annual trade and commerce for Norfolk's present population, of which we hereafter make note.

POPULATION AND EXPANSION.

From official reports of the United States census office, we find the population, as enumerated for Norfolk city in 1890, given at 34,986, and Portsmouth at 12,345. In 1870 the population of Norfolk was stated to be 19,229, in 1880 at 21,966, and with the figures given as above, 34,986 for 1890, our percentage of increase shows 14 per cent. for the first decade and 59.27 per cent. for the last.

This increase is not surprising when we find the old city covered with stores and dwellings in almost every available space, and the suburbs for three miles out in every direction selling at $1,000 to $1,500 per acre, and lots 25x110 selling readily at $250 to $800 each within easy access to the city.

"Observer," in the Norfolk *Virginian*, of recent date, has this to say about the present situation:

A few years ago a land boomer would probably describe Lambert's Point as a locality where all facilities existed, and where every imaginable opportunity was at hand to aid the purposes of commerce. This description would probably, at that time, compel some people to shrug their shoulders, shake their heads and express themselves in a manner not at all complimentary to the predictions of real estate agents; but to-day the wharves of Lambert's Point are crowded with shipping, which carry from our shores the products of the Sunny South. That Norfolk has made wonderful progress in the onward march of cities of the south is palpable to anybody who has lived here for any lengthened period. Let a person, after an absence of some years, revisit Norfolk. Palatial residences have sprung up and superseded very modest buildings where our visitor perhaps at one time slept peacefully, perfectly unconscious of future changes, and so remarkable and varied have been the improvements that if he were possessed of a good imagination he would come to the conclusion that Norfolk was endeavoring to disguise herself through the instrumentality of architectural changes from the admiring gaze of her old citizens.

INDUCEMENTS TO MANUFACTURERS.

Because Norfolk is a seaport city why is she not a desirable location for manufacturing plants?

. A glance at our statistics will show that we have at hand all the lumber, coal and iron at first hands and in abundant quantities.

On the line of three of our railroads, penetrating southwest and west Virginia, hard woods and those suitable for the construction of domestic wares—especially furniture—may be found in great abundance, and transported to this city at a minimum expense.

A belt line railroad around this harbor, and soon to be built, will give equal facilities to five railroads, already here, to deliver as well as receive freight at the doors of the factory for shipment over land or water to any portion of the country.

Recent investments in land around Norfolk, by home and foreign capitalists, have enabled them to offer sites for manufacturing plants upon the most favorable terms; and through a Promoting and Investment Company, organized under a liberal charter, are ready to lend or invest in the establishing of manufacturing industries.

Letters of enquiry will receive prompt attention if addressed to the Secretary of the Chamber of Commerce.

PHYSICAL AND FINANCIAL GROWTH.

The reader of these pages cannot fail to realize that there has been a marked material development in this ancient city within the last ten years, and that the forces now at work will necessarily bring a more wonderful increase within the next decade.

It has been our aim to place only facts before the public, as they are, that far-seeing men may calculate the profits which judicious investments are sure to bring in the near future. With the advent of the current year a notable demand was observed for city and suburban property, and gradually the figures paid were startling. Property on or near the water front, within three to five miles above and below the city found ready buyers at $500 to $1,500 per acre, about ten times the price at which they could have been bought two years ago.

This activity, not yet at the flood, has been stimulated by our growth in trade relations with other sections through railroad extensions, and the development by trunk lines concentrating in this harbor. Capitalists from the money centres in this country and in Europe have placed, and are placing their capital here in vast sums, thus showing their confidence in the belief that Norfolk, with its great harbor and location, is about to attain the destiny which many great and wise men have in the past predicted for her.

The following figures will illustrate the movement in property transfers for the current year :

TRANSACTIONS IN REAL ESTATE IN NORFOLK COUNTY, AND THE CITIES OF NORFOLK AND PORTSMOUTH DURING THE YEAR 1890, ARE RECORDED AS FOLLOWS:

In Norfolk County	$3,801,063 00
In Norfolk City	2,540,635 00
In Portsmouth City	734,900 00
Total	$7,076,598 00

It is estimated that the sales of land in Norfolk County for the year, and represented in the above table, reached about 8,500 acres.

ASSESSMENT OF REAL ESTATE IN NORFOLK CITY FOR THE YEAR 1890 COMPARED WITH THAT MADE IN 1885.

IN 1890.

NORFOLK CITY (FOUR OLD WARDS.)

Value of land	$ 9,435,661
Value of buildings	7,124,688
	$16,560,349

ATLANTIC CITY WARD.

Value of land	$ 1,419,180
Value of buildings	151,250
	$ 1,570,430

BRAMBLETON WARD.

Value of land...$ 1,237,191
Value of buildings...557,220

$ 1,794,411

Total value of land..$42,092,032
Total value of buildings..7,833,158

$49,925,190
Assessed value of real estate in city of Norfolk.................$49,925,190

COMPARED WITH 1885.

Four old wards, new assessment...$16,560,349
Four old wards, old assessment...12,307,130

Increase in five years in four wards...$ 4,253,219
Add new assessment in the new wards, given above in detail......3,364,841

Total increase of taxable values in five years.........................$ 7,618,060

The following is a comparative statement of the taxable values as between 1890 and the assessment for 1891:

Four wards (new assessment for 1891)....................................$16,560,349
Taxable real estate value 1890..12,785,385

Increase...$ 3,774,954
Brambleton (new assessments for 1891)....................................1,794,411
Assessments 1890...1,082,720

Increase...$ 711,691
Atlantic City (new assessment for 1889)...................................$ 1,570,430
Assessments 1889..57,370

Increase...$ 1,633,060

Total increase of the assessment for 1891 over values of 1890.........$ 5,549,505
Total state and city taxes, $2.20 per $100 of value, (city $1.60, water 20c. state 40c.)

CITY REVENUE COMPARED.

	For taxes.	Licenses.
In 1890	$285,556.31	$74,677.84
In 1884	236,352.64	54,087.90
Increase	$49,203.67	$20,589.94

NORFOLK'S ACREAGE.

Prior to the annexation of the two Wards now known as Brambleton and Atlantic City, the acreage of the city was, upon the authority of City Engineer W. T. Brooke, 880 acres. In 1887 Brambleton added 340 acres, and in 1890 Atlantic City gave an additional 1,250 acres. Total acreage of the present city is therefore 2,470, or within a fraction of four square miles.

OUR RAILROADS AND THEIR CONNECTIONS.

The following railroads, alphabetically arranged, practically terminate in Norfolk. Those that have planted their depots in the suburbs reach the city by their own special ferry and barge connections:

THE ATLANTIC AND DANVILLE RAILROAD,

from Portsmouth to Danville, Va., via Suffolk, Franklin, Courtland and Belfield, to Danville, Va., and now extending their line west of the latter city to Bristol, Tenn.

THE CHESAPEAKE AND OHIO RAILROAD,

from Norfolk by steamer to Newport News, thence to Richmond, Charlottsville, Staunton, the principal Virginia and West Virginia springs, Huntington, Cincinnati, Louisville, Chicago, and all points west and southwest, and connects with the Southern Pacific railroad.

THE EASTERN CAROLINA DISPATCH,

from Norfolk to Newberne, Kinston, Goldsboro, and all points reached by the Atlantic and North Carolina railroad by steamer to Washington, N. C., and landings on the Tar river.

THE NORFOLK AND WESTERN RAILROAD,

from Norfolk to Suffolk, Petersburg, Lynchburg, Roanoke, Bristol, and all points south and west via East Tennessee, Virginia and Georgia railroad, with connections at Suffolk with the Seaboard and Roanoke, the Atlantic and Danville, Norfolk and Carolina, and west as far as Kansas City. Other connections at Waverly with the Atlantic and Danville railroad; at Petersburg with the Atlantic Coast Line; At Lynchburg with the Virginia Midland; at Roanoke with Shenandoah Valley; at Burkville with Richmond and Danville. Extensions from Radford to Pocahontas; from Pulaski City to Ivanhoe; from Glade Spring to Saltville.

THE NORFOLK AND CAROLINA,

from Norfolk to Tarboro, a part of the Atlantic Coast Line system, reaching via Tarboro, Goldsboro Wilson, Fayetteville and Raleigh, Wilmington, Charleston, Savannah, and points in South Carolina, Florida and Georgia, with branches to Scotland Neck, Greenville, Plymouth and Kinston, N. C., connecting with all points on the Wilmington and Weldon Railroad.

THE NEW YORK, PHILADELPHIA AND NORFOLK,

via Cape Charles to Wilmington, Chester, Philadelphia and New York. All interior Delaware, New Jersey and Pennsylvania points, with connections east and west over the Pennsylvania railroad, of which this is a favorable connection.

THE SEABOARD AIR LINE SYSTEM OF RAILROADS

is composed of the Seaboard and Roanoke, Raleigh and Gaston, Raleigh and

Augusta, Carolina Central, Durham and Northern and Georgia, Carolina and Northern Railroads, with branches from Franklinton to Louisburg, N. C., from Moncure to Pittsborough; from Cameron to Carthage, and from Hamlet to Gibsons, and gives Norfolk direct connections with Weldon, Henderson, Durham, Raleigh and all points on the Cape Fear and Yadkin Valley Railroad, Wadesboro, Monroe, Charlotte, Lincolnton, Shelby and Rutherfordton, N. C., and Chester, Clinton, Greenwood and Abbeville, S. C.; also Augusta, Atlanta and Macon, Ga., and all parts in the South.

THE NORFOLK SOUTHERN RAILROAD,

from Norfolk to Elizabeth City, connecting with steamers for the Pesquotank and Alligator Rivers. At Edenton, steamer Plymouth for all points on the Roanoke River and by steamer Roberts for all points on the Scuppernong and Chowan Rivers.

THE OCEAN VIEW RAILROAD.

This road runs from Norfolk to Ocean View, a favorite summer resort on the Chesapeake Bay, eight miles from the city. A good hotel, fine bathing and fishing, and many thousands frequent it from May to September.

THE VIRGINIA BEACH RAILROAD.

From Norfolk, eighteen miles to the Atlantic Ocean, at Virginia Beach, five miles south of Cape Henry. The finest sand beach on the coast only a hundred yards from the hotel piazza. Surf bathing in all its purity and stimulating effects, fishing, hunting and boating on the lake immediately in rear of hotel. Beautiful shade, lovely promenading grounds and numerous private cottages.

OCEAN, BAY AND RIVER LINES.

The following lines by water transportation have a home in this Harbor and for many years identified with this port. Many of them have grown from small beginnings to great power and wealth through their connections with our railroads which transfer both ways their freights to destination:

The BAY LINE, from Norfolk to Baltimore,
WILLIAM RANDALL, Agent.

The OLD DOMINION S. S. CO., from Norfolk to New York,
CULPEPER & TURNER, Agents.

The CLYDE LINE, from Philadelphia to Norfolk,
JAS. W. McCAARICK, Agent.

The CLYDE NORTH CAROLINA LINE,
JAS. W. McCARRICK, Agent.

The OLD DOMINION AND NORTH CAROLINA LINE,
CULPEPER & TURNER, Agents.

The OLD DOMINION VIRGINIA LINE,
CULPEPER & TURNER, Agents.

The MERCHANTS AND MINERS TRANSPORTATION CO,
RICHARD H. WRIGHT, Agent.

The VIRGINIA STEAMBOAT CO.,
JAS. W. McCARRICK, Agent.

The INLAND SEABOARD COASTING CO., to Washington, D. C,
JAS. W. McCARRICK, Agent.

The POTOMAC STEAMBOAT CO., to Washington, D. C.,
V. D. GRONER, Agent.

The PETERSBURG AND NORFOLK STEAMBOAT CO.,
W. L. WILKINSON, Agent.

Numerous other lines navigating the waters of Virginia, and penetrating North Carolina, are known as Bennett's, Jones', Harbinger's, Johnson's, Roanoke, Norfolk and Baltimore, etc., forming close connection with scores of towns and villages having Norfolk as their trading point.

CANALS.

The Albermarle and Chesapeake Canal, with only one lock, 210x40 feet, connecting this port with the rivers and sounds of North Carolina through to Florida, is a valuable feeder, and brings to this market millions of tonnage of lumber and farm products that cannot otherwise reach or bear land transportation. FRANKLIN WELD, President.

A TOWN IN 1680---A BOROUGH IN 1736---A CITY IN 1845.

From the fourth edition of "Norfolk as a Business Centre," issued in 1884, we learn that the name Norfolk was originally bestowed upon the district, afterwards county, by one Col. Thorogood, one of the earliest settlers, in honor of his native country in England, and a similar sentiment of patriotism would appear to have suggested the designation of other towns and localities in Virginia which abounds in names borrowed from the mother country. We learn, also, from the same source, that the General Assembly of the State in 1680 authorized the purchase of fifty acres of land for the "town" of Norfolk, and in pursuance of this authority a tract which forms the northwestern portion of the present city was purchased in 1682 for 10,000 pounds of tobacco, from Nicholas Wise, a carpenter, whose father had acquired some reputation as a local ship builder.

From that time forward the town appears to have enjoyed a long period of almost uninterrupted prosperity, during which the population continued to increase and multiply and her commercial influence to expand, for in September, 1736, she was formally incorporated by Royal Charter, as a Borough, with a mayor, recorder and eight aldermen.

Such has been written of the early history of Norfolk. Her share of the horrors of the revolution, and the war of 1812, are matters of history, and need not be repeated here.

In 1787 a charter was obtained by the States of Virginia and North Carolina under which the Dismal Swamp Canal was commenced in 1787, and opened for navigation in 1828. In 1801 the navy yard on the Portsmouth side of our inner harbor was established, the land being ceded by the Governor of Virginia to the United States Government by authority of the General Assembly. In 1804 Tom Moore, "Erin's sweetest poet," visited Norfolk, and subsequently embalmed in verse the famous "Lake Drummond, That Mighty Reservoir of Water in the Great Dismal Swamp."

The visit of General Lafayette to Norfolk in 1824 was the occasion of much social entertainment, and great honors were paid to this conspicuous friend of the American Republic.

The centennial of Norfolk's incorporation as a Borough was duly celebrated in 1836, and on February 13th, 1845, by an act of the General Assembly, Norfolk's charter was amended and she became a city with all its honors, privileges and responsibilities.

AS SEEN BY OTHER EYES THAN OURS.

So much has been written by non-residents of Norfolk to the journals of other cities, about its growth and prospects, and the abundant opportunities here for the investment of capital, that we have been constrained to reproduce a few of these letters to give additional force to what we have ourselves written. Disinterested praise will go further with some readers than that which has the suspicion of self-interest.

We, therefore, commend these letters to the careful perusal of every one who turns these pages for light and information about Norfolk and its vicinity.

THE HARBOR OF NORFOLK.—Lieu't. Henry H. Barroll, U. S. N., in charge of the branch Hydrographic office in Norfolk, has, by special request, contributed to this report an article upon the harbor of Norfolk. Of course, the writer, who is a keen observer and has had experience, by reason of his position and intellectual attainments in various portions of the world, sees, and is willing to commit to print his own impressions of this great harbor.

CHARTERS
—FOR—
LAND AND IMPROVEMENT COMPANIES.

In the Corporation and Circuit Court records for the city we find the following Charters granted during the year 1890. All enquiries addressed to the Presidents of these Companies at the Norfolk P. O. will receive prompt reply :

NAME OF COMPANY.	CAPITAL.	PRESIDENT.
The Atlantic Improvement Co.,	$ 50,000 00	D. Lowenberg.
The Atlantic and Chesapeake Real Estate Association,	500,000 00	W. D. Pender.
The Atlantic City Improvement Co.,	50,000 00	L. H. Shields.
The Brambleton Heights Co.,	50,000 00	L. H. Shields.
The Bedford Park Land Co.,	100,000 00	Walter F. Irvine.
The Bedford City Development Co.,	100,000 00	O. M. Styron.
The Chesapeake Land Co.,	50,000 00	Foster Black.
The Commonwealth Realty Co.,	300,000 00	A. E Campe.
The Central Land Co.,	175,000 00	J. A. Welch.
The Cape Henry Park and Land Co.,	300,000 00	R. H. Baker.
The Eureka Co.,	25,000 00	Fergus Reid.
The Eastern Branch Improvement Co.,	100,000 00	W. A. Wrenn.
The East Norfolk Land and Improvement Co.,	50,000 00	F. D. Pinkerton.
The Elizabeth Land and Improvement Co.,	300,000 00	William Pannill.
The East Virginia Land and Improvement Co.,	100,000 00	George D. Pleasant.
The Glasgow Development Co.,	750 000 00	Barton Myers.
The Investment Co., of Norfolk,	300,000 00	Barton Myers.
The Lambert's Point Improvement Co.,	25,000 00	C. W. Fentress.
The Lambert's Point Co.,	200,000 00	William Lamb.
The Lambert's Point Land and Development Co.,	100,000 00	Granville Gaines,
The Lambert's Point Development Co.,	100,000 00	W. R. Marberry.
The Lambert's Point Co of Norfolk,	300,000 00	Barton Myers.
The Land Investment Co., of Norfolk,	300 000 00	C. A. Nash.
The Lambert's Point Water Front Co.,	300,000 00	Barton Myers.
The Lambert's Point Land Co.,	75,000 00	William Lamb.
The North Brook Land Co.,	100,000 00	George R. Dunn.
The Norfolk Co.,	5,000,000 00	John H. Dingee.
The Norfolk Water Front Development Co.,	300,000 00	Barton Myers.

NAME OF COMPANY.	CAPITAL.	PRESIDENT.
The Norfolk and Lambert's Point Land Co.,	100,000 00	B. Moormaw.
The Norfolk Manufacturing Co.,	50,000 00	E. Campe.
The Norfolk Investment Co.,	50,000 00	E. V. White.
The North Norfolk Co.,	500,000 00	Jno. M. Littig.
The Norfolk Suburban Land Co.,	15,000 00	H. L. Page.
The National Investment Co.,	300,000 00	Geo. T. Scott.
The Norfolk Industrial Development Co.,	1,000,000 00	Barton Myers.
The Norfolk and Lambert's Point Co.,	100,000 00	L. H. Shields.
The North Roanoke Land and Improvement Co.,	50,000 00	Jas. S. Simmons.
The Norfolk Rolleston Co.	50,000 00	Jas. W. Gerow.
The Norfolk and Eastern Investment Co.,	1,000,000 00	John Q. Hoyt.
The Northeast Norfolk Land Co.,	500,000 00	M. Umstadter.
The Norfolk Development Co.,	100,000 00	L. D. Smith.
The Norfolk Terminal Land Co.,	500,000 00	J. T. Fitzgerald.
The Old Dominion Investment Co., of Newport News,	100,000 00	L. P. Stearnes.
The River Front Land Co.	100,000 00	V. D. Groner.
The River View Land Co.,	150,000 00	Charles R. Nash.
The Rock Creek Co.,	150,000 00	T. S Garnett.
The South Norfolk Land Co.,	50,000 00	C. G. Joynes.
The South Portsmouth Land and Improvement Co.,	50,000 00	F. Richardson.
The Seaboard Land and Development Co.,	100,000 00	Walter Sharp.
The Safety Land Co.,	200,000 00	Thos. Pannill
The South Border Investment Co.,	300,000 00	J. Taylor Ellyson.
The South Norfolk Investment Co.,	300,000 00	J. W. Perry.
The Virginia and Kentucky Improvement Co.,	50,000 00	Barton Myers.
The Virginia Investment Co.,	20,000 00	E. V. White.
The Virginia Land Co. of Bedford,	150,000 00	Mills L. Eure.
The West Atlantic City Land Co.,	25,000 00	Fred M. Killam.
The West Portsmouth Land Co.,	50,000 00	F. Richardson.
The West End Real Estate Co., of Norfolk,	300,000 00	Geo. R. Dunn.

HYGIENE AND CLIMATIC CONDITIONS.

By special request the following article is furnished for publication in this report. It is prepared with care by a close student and observer of all matters relating to hygienic and climatology, whose able help was invited by the late Dr. A. Y. P. Garnett, U. S. A., at Washington, D. C., to furnish the data for this portion of tidewater Virginia for the American Climatological Society in 1888.

Dr. Jackson has resided in Norfolk for twenty-five years, and enjoys a large practice, and a high place in the profession, as a man of learning and scientific attainments.

As ex-President and Honorary Fellow of the Virginia State Medical Society, member of the American Medical Association and of the Ninth International Medical Congress, he is fully qualified to treat of the matters which are herewith furnished in behalf of his adopted home.

NORFOLK, VA., December 15th, 1890.

SAMUEL R. BORUM, ESQ.,

Secretary and Superintendent Chamber of Commerce :

MY DEAR SIR:—I, with pleasure, comply with your request to furnish you such facts with regard to the climate and health of Norfolk, as may be "of interest to persons at a distance who may contemplate a removal to this city for business or pleasure."

To do this seems hardly necessary at this time, for, judging from the crowds of people who frequent our places of resort, it might be supposed that our delightful climate was appreciated, and that our northern friends had become satisfied as to the healthfulness of this locality.

Persons living in the same latitude as Norfolk, but at a distance from the Atlantic coast, could hardly realize and, without a study of the causes, would find it difficult to understand the mildness of our climate as compared with their own.

The influence of the water is well understood here, for vegetation is much earlier on those farms which are directly located on the edge of streams; and for trucking purposes, such farms are always most in demand.

It may be asked "Why has the water so much effect on the climate and vegetation?" It is owing not so much to our proximity to the Gulf Stream as it is to the eddies from that great "ocean river," which are caused by the impediment to the northward flow of its western edge, which is produced by the great rush of water from the Chesapeake Bay and from all of its tributaries through the narrow gate-way between the Virginia capes. This immense body of water must have sufficient momentum to force it far out to sea, and thus by heading off the current of the western (which in this latitude is the warmer) edge of the Gulf Stream, it causes a reflection of this warm water to our coast and into all the bays and estuaries with which it is indented. This is the reason why such myriads of wild fowl, ducks, geese and swan migrate to this region on the appearance of winter. And the migration of these birds, one might suppose, would furnish a suggestion to human beings as to the best localities for resort in order to escape the rigors of winter. The Gulf Stream is nearer to the American coast between Capes Hatteras and Henry than anywhere else, and this proximity, together with the eddies above alluded to, afford a satisfactory explanation of the mildness of our climate.

After leaving the Virginia capes this mysterious current trends rapidly to the east, until when opposite the New Jersey coast it is four or five times the distance from its shore than it is from the Virginia coast. The farther north it goes the greater its divergence from the American shore, and after more than 2,000 miles of travel, during which it must have spent a large amount of its heat, it reaches the Irish coast with sufficient warmth retained to render that far off northern region the beautiful green spot that it is. But for the heat derived from this source, instead of being the "Emerald Isle," Ireland would be as cold and barren as Labrador or Greenland. But the genial influence of the Gulf Stream is felt even still further north than this. It can be traced as far as the coast of Norway, upon which it has made possible the location of the most northerly city on the globe, (Hammerfest) in latitude 70° 40'. the water of whose harbor is never frozen.

It can readily be understood, then, that such a region, with a climate so mild as seldom to be colder than 16° above zero, where ice but seldom forms, where snow, if it falls at all, lies but a few hours on the ground ; a region, almost surrounded by water which has been warmed, as explained above: by water whose vapor is surcharged with oxygen ; a region contiguous to the great cypress and juniper forests of the Dismal Swamp, and to the ozone-producing pine forests of tide water Virginia and eastern North Carolina, and finally that such a region would be a most favorable locality for persons liable to pulmonary disease. However much the highlands of Colorado may be vaunted as the place for consumptives, my own experience warrants me in declaring that I would rather take my chances here than so close to the line of perpetual snow as are those elevated localities, and I believe we can furnish a better showing than they in the treatment of this class of diseases.

It is well known to us that Norfolk has had the reputation abroad of being an unhealthy place. This impression, as unreasonable as it is unfortunate, was produced by a sickness among some troops who, during the war of 1812, were stationed at what was then a very unhealthy locality some miles from Norfolk, and also by the disastrous importation of yellow fever in 1855, by which latter epidemic the city lost some two thousand of her inhabitants. This would have ruined the prospects of Norfolk but for the fact that it was known that the disease was imported and had not been generated here; and further, that the subsequent winter proved sufficiently severe to destroy the last vestige of the disease so that it has never revived since, and will never reappear unless through carelessness or inadvertence of the health authorities.

That Norfolk suffered many years ago from malarial diseases cannot be doubted, and a little reflection and a comparison of the condition of things at that time with that of the present, will explain the cause of the prevalence then as well as the present immunity from this class of diseases.

When Norfolk was first located, as is the case with every town near the water, the higher points of land nearest the water's edge were selected for occupation. The desire for water fronts caused the city to grow mostly at the water's edge. The filling up of low places at the shore cut off from the tide depressions away from the water, and converted what had been inlets into stagnant ponds, and these furnished the most favorable nidi for the malarial poison. Since the city has grown beyond these ponds and has reached the higher background these sources of infection are entirely removed, and at this time it may be safely declared that the malarial poison is not generated within the city limits, and, indeed, for some distance beyond.

It has been my habit for some years to inquire into the history of every case of malarial fever occurring in my practice, and it is seldom the case that I fail to trace the disease to some locality distant from the city. Not only has the filling up of the depressions alluded to contributed largely to the health of the city, but also the admirable system of sewerage, which has only been completed within two years, has had much to do in diminishing the death rate, which, at this time, compares most favorably with the healthiest cities of this or any other country. In corroboration of this statement let us refer to the statistics of the past year, which is really the first year the sewerage could have had effect upon the health of the city.

The number of deaths per thousand of population for the year ending July 1st, 1890, was 21.77; of whites the number per thousand for the same period was 16.90; of colored, 28.22 per thousand. The large excess of deaths among the colored people is well understood by those who are familiar with their mode of life. Their uncleanly habits, the want of ventilation, and the total exclusion of sunlight from their dwellings are the chief factors in causing the production of their high death rate. For these reasons the death rate of the whites should only enter into the calculation; and this we see is now at the low rate of 16.5 per thousand for the year 1890.

Let us now sum up the conditions which are found to exist here, and which render Norfolk not only a desirable and pleasant place of residence, but also a valuable health resort.

1st. A comparatively equable climate, with less range of temperature than any locality east of the Rocky Mountains

2d. A delightful winter climate, about the temperature of Georgia or northern Louisiana, having about the same winter isotherm as Shreveport.

3d. A delightful summer climate, so cooled by the southeast sea breeze as to make our summer isotherm about that of Kansas City. There is no need of leaving Norfolk in order to escape the heat of summer. I have suffered more from heat in New York than I have ever done in Norfolk.

4th. The prevalence of sea breezes containing an excess of oxygen, which are peculiarly grateful, valuable and beneficial to those consumptives who suffer from dyspnœa.

5th. Our proximity to the great pine forests of eastern Virginia and North Carolina, which are found to be generators of ozone, (an allotropic form of oxygen) one of the most valuable conditions for consumptives.

6th. Our proximity to the Gulf Stream, which contributes to our charming winter, not only by the breezes which, after being warmed by its surface bears its delightful temperature to us, but also by its eddies which actually lave our shores.

7th. Our winter climate, though not severe, is sufficiently cold to destroy disease-producing germs, for in no instance has yellow fever been known to live through the winter so as to revive on the reappearance of warm weather.

In addition to what I have written here I beg leave to refer you to a communication contributed by me at the request of a committee of the American Climotological Association, which is included in the report of Dr. A. Y. P. Garnett, of Washington, to that national society.

These papers discuss the points contained in this communication more fully than I have been able to do at this time, and in addition furnish most interesting and valuable comparisons of the climate of Norfolk with that of other points on the Atlantic coast.

Hoping that this may serve your purpose, and will direct attention to this, the finest climate east of the Rocky Mountains, I am

Yours truly,   S. K. JACKSON, M. D.

P. S.

Since writing the above I happened to glance at the weather map issued by the signal bureau for this day, December 18th, which so fully confirms the assertions made by me that I cannot forbear extending my communication for the purpose of copying from it some of its figures. I wish I could reproduce the whole map.

The isothermal line passing through Norfolk is marked 40°; after leaving this city it passes through the following places, at all of which the temperature is just the same, viz , 40°: First Lynchburg, then it dips south and passes off the coast above Wilmington, N. C., (which is 38°) then sweeps to S. W., crosses Florida south of Jacksonville, (which is 38°) then west across the northern edge of the Gulf of Mexico, strikes the land between New Orleans (44°) and Mobile, (32°) rises toward the northwest through Shreveport, dips rapidly south into Texas considerably to the east of Rio Grande City, whose temperature is as low as 34°, 6° below Norfolk's. This map enables us to compare Norfolk's temperature with other cities to the south of us and the statement may astonish those who have not paid attention to this subject. The temperature of Norfolk and all the places mentioned as being on the same isothermal line is 40°, Wilmington, N. C., 38°; Charleston, S. C., 38°; Augusta, 38°; Atlanta, 32°; Savannah, 38°; Jacksonville, 38°; Montgomery, 32°; Meridian, 32°; Vicksburg, 30°; Memphis, 34°; Cairo, in the same latitude as Norfolk, 28°; Nashville, 36°; Knoxville, 32°; Charlotte, 38°; Mobile, 32°. The only localities recorded as higher than Norfolk are Hatteras, 42 °; Titusville, Fla., 42°; Jupiter, in southern part of Florida, 48°; New Orleans, 44°; San Antonia, 48°; Corpus Christi, 42°; Brownsville, 46°; Palestine, La., 46°.

This is a most remarkable showing, but the same may be seen to be the case often during the winter.

On this day, December 18th, 1890, whose record is given above, occurred the clearing up of a N. E. storm, which was hardly recognized as such at Norfolk. But little rain and no snow fell during its passage over us, while some 100 or 150 miles to the west of us the severest snow storm occurred since that of 1857. While we have not seen a flake of snow we see accounts of the crushing in of houses, of the blocking up of roads, and of numerous houses snowed in, from the Shenandoah Valley and west to the Ohio river.

On the coast to the north of us immense damage is reported, as on the New Jersey coast, at Long Branch, Asbury Park and Atlantic City. Houses are reported to be either surrounded by water or washed out to sea, and large portions of the several health resorts are reported submerged. Truly we have cause to be thankful, for no such disaster on our coast has been reported.

Equally interesting and important is another report which has just been brought to my attention. It contains some statistics furnished by Rev. Dr. Barten, on the occurrence of the twenty-fifth anniversary of his rectorship of Christ Church. Though it is the report of but one parish, it may be taken as an index of all others in the city, and is well worth reproducing:

In the twenty-five years there were 1,152 funerals, as follows: Under 1 year, 214; 1 to 10, 155; 10 to 20, 39; 20 to 30, 110; 30 to 40, 128; 40 to 50, 130; 50 to 60, 115; 60 to 70, 96; 70 to 80, 103; 81 to 90, 52; 90 to 92, 2; 94 to 95, 1; 96, 1; 98, 1; 99, 1. By this showing of the 1,152 deaths, 165 of them were persons over 70 years of age, or 14.3 per cent.

This is a most favorable exhibit, and needs no comment.

S. K. JACKSON, M. D.

COAST DEFENSES---CHESAPEAKE BAY.

BY HON. MARSHALL PARKS

Since the introduction of modern war ships and heavy ordnance our old-fashioned stone forts are no longer able to defend the seaport cities, and they are at the mercy of any second rate power.

The defense of the Chesapeake is the only protection to our national capital and the numerous cities and towns that are on the rivers that flow into the Bay. It would seem, therefore, that the proper place for defence should

be at the "gates of the ocean." Cape Henry and Cape Charles are only ten
miles apart, but there are many shoals on the Cape Charles side, and heavy
laden ships must enter near Cape Henry. It is proposed to remove the Rip
Raps, Fort (Calhoun-Wool,) as it is no longer necessary for an adjunct to
Fortress Monroe, and transplant it on the middle ground between Cape
Henry and Cape Charles, about six miles distant from the former, and erect
upon it a modern steel clad structure, mounted with the heaviest guns, and
so arranged to furnish shelter for a few small torpedo boats; to build at Cape
Henry earth works fortifications and unite them with submarine cables having all the latest appliances for submarine batteries. ˙ Lynn Haven river, close
under Cape Henry, may be made a central station for torpedo boats to assist
in the defence.

Should the enemy attempt to land any where south along the coast, by the
construction of a few short canals and removal of a few shoals in the natural
waterways, these torpedoes and mortar boats may proceed as far south as
Florida without going one mile in the ocean.

If the mortar and torpedo boats should be required north they may proceed up Chesapeake Bay and through the Chesapeake and Delaware Canal to
Philadelphia and thence by Delaware and Raritan Canal to New York and,
if required on the Lakes, go to Oswego or Buffalo by the Erie Canal.

The old tower formerly used as a light-house at Cape Henry could have
an electric search light placed upon it.

THE HARBOR OF NORFOLK, VIRGINIA.

BY HENRY H. BARROLL, LIEU'T. U. S. NAVY.

Norfolk, owing to its fortunate geographical position, is necessarily one of
the most important shipping points on the Atlantic coast. As regards safety
and facility of access, it has no superior among the Northern ports; while
those farther southward do not in any degree compare with it in either of the
above advantages.

The Gulf Stream, transporting immense volumes of tropically heated
water, flowing north, is breasted off to the eastward by Cape Hatteras,
Experience shows that the cyclonic storms, occurring during the months of
July, August and September, have a tendency to re-curve to the eastward in
latitudes varying from 28° to 32° north—Cape Hatteras being in about 35°,
and Cape Henry in about 37°, north latitude.

The warm atmosphere resting above the surface of the Gulf Stream is met
by the cold air-walls, borne in waves from the northwest, producing gales,
squalls or stormy weather; and causing the passage of Cape Hatteras to be
generally attended with more or less difficulty and danger.

Norfolk furnishes the first secure harbor to the northward of this cape, and also a safe outlet through which all of the vast inland commerce, arriving from below this point, may seek the ocean.

Water carriage will ever hold the supremacy over transportation by any other means. As regards her advantages in this respect, Norfolk can claim to be one of the most favored cities in the United States.

The broad entrance to Chesapeake Bay, a body of water which, for commercial purposes has no equal, allows vessels under either steam or sail to readily enter Hampton Roads, where is found the largest and safest harbor south of New York. The James and Elizabeth rivers, here meeting, form a triangular estuary in which large fleets of merchant shipping may, throughout the most violent gales, safely ride at anchor.

There is a 26-foot channel, well marked with buoys and lighthouses, and varying in width from 100 to 1,000 yards, which leads from the entrance of Chesapeake Bay to the wharves of Norfolk, and also beyond, to the United States Navy Yard. It is well to particularly notice this, since, notwithstanding the dredging of this channel at great expense, by the national government, still foreign shippers are not generally aware of its existence.

There are thirty-two pilots allowed by the state law, and the authorized pilotage is smaller than that of any other port in the United States, being from $2.50 to $4.50 per foot, according to the vessel's draught.

Two important water-ways—the Dismal Swamp Canal and the Albermarle and Chesapeake Canal—connect the North Carolina Sounds with Chesapeake Bay, making a part of that system of inland navigation which extends from Beaufort and Newberne, North Carolina, to Baltimore, Philadelphia, New York, and if so desired, to the great Northern Lakes.

These water-ways are arteries, through which flow from the Albermarle and Pamplico Sounds, and their tributary streams, the varied commercial products of Eastern North Carolina, and territory even farther south and west.

Until our attention is directed to this fact, we fail to realize the extent to which these inland passages are used; but a glance at the statistics of Norfolk's lumber and stave trade will give an idea of their importance, when we reflect that, substantially, the entire supply of timber introduced into the Norfolk market, may be said to arrive through these canals.

Huge rafts, like immense serpents, wind along, each in tow of a diminitive tug, the total expense of which, though slight, is yet sufficient to allow a fair profit to the raftsmen as well as to the lumber dealer; while the tugs return, having in tow, long lines of schooners loaded with farming machinery and other manufactured articles from the workshops of Norfolk and cities further north.

The James River and Chesapeake Bay naturally deliver their produce at Norfolk. These, with their tributary streams, represent a total length of 1,500 miles of tidal coast. That of the North Carolina Sounds further augments this to about 2,500 miles of coast line which, although inland water, is yet daily washed and purified by the salt waves.

The climate is such an equable one that the three neighboring seaside resorts, Old Point Comfort, Virginia Beach and Ocean View, may well declare themselves to be either winter or summer resorts. The thermometer in summer ranges between 70° and 90° Fahr., and in winter rarely falls below 20°.

The mean annual rainfall is about 52 inches, fairly distributed throughout the year, about 35 inches being precipitated during that period extending from the 1st of March to the 1st of October, the time when the crops are growing. Possibly it is due to this tempering of the climate by the Gulf Stream, and also to the certainty of an abundance of rain when most needed, that Norfolk has become a great trucking centre on the Atlantic coast. Be the cause what it may, those persons who have visited all parts of the globe concur in asserting that here is found a market which is equal to, if not superior, to any other market in the world. The market for vegetables, game, poultry and fish is always excellent.

The oyster interest of Chesapeake Bay, though much deteriorated in later years, owing to injudicious dredging and insufficient protection, is now being better guarded through stringent laws enacted by those states whose interests have been so jeopardized, and oyster planting is now being largely resorted to in order to replace the devastation of the natural beds. Oyster culture is more profitable, acre for acre, than the raising of any other article of food. Norfolk is the natural centre for this trade, so far as the waters of the Chesapeake Bay and its tributaries are concerned, and has for her only rival the city of Baltimore, a place more difficult of access to the oysterman.

Already Lambert's Point and Newport News have become the greatest coaling stations on the Atlantic coast, while the grade of coal here handled, "Pocahontas" produces the finest steaming results, and is preferred by the ocean greyhounds in making their great transatlantic races.

The United States Navy Yard, with its two dry docks and modern steel-working machinery, and the recently established ship building plant at Newport's News, with a dry dock of greater capacity than any other in America, give an assurance of having at all times, in this vicinity plenty of skilled workmen and the proper facilities for docking and repairing the largest ocean steamships.

Norfolk stands where each of the several lines of railroad, leading from the south and west, finds its earliest and most reliable seaboard terminus.

Although large cities are sometimes found located inland, as London, Paris, etc., yet history shows it to be the invariable rule that at those points where there are good harbors, or where large water courses meet the ocean, great and populous cities will be established. Norfolk possesses both of these advantages, and her fine harbor, with its tributary water communication, assures to her the fact that she will in the future become the largest city of the South.

VIRGINIA'S HISTORIC CITY.

BY A SPECIAL CORRESPONDENT OF THE NEW YORK EVENING POST, JUNE 25th, 1890.

Southern "booms" are suggestive of artificiality in many cases. But the good old town of Norfolk, Virginia, which is renewing its youth nowadays in a particularly lusty and aggressive manner, cannot be suspected of employing the tricks of the professional boomer's trade. Its age protects its reputation, and furthermore, the evidences of the solidity of its boom are too many and obvious to be gainsaid or belittled.

There is no reason why Norfolk should not become speedily one of the largest, richest and most important cities of the United States. In fact, in the writer's opinion—which is the opinion of a disinterested New Yorker who has had occasion to visit Norfolk several times within the last few years, and to observe its growth during that period—Virginia's historic "City by the Sea" is under full headway towards the realization of that possibility.

THE NATURAL ADVANTAGES

in its favor are known to the nation, but not so well known or appreciated as they might be; and what has been done in the recent past in the line of commercial and social advance is worthy of attention from the business men and capitalists of the North.

Norfolk is the leading seaport of Virginia, and by nature was fitted and intended for the chief seaport of the South. Its harbor is the best in all respects on the Atlantic coast, south of New York, and in one important respect is superior to that of New York—it has no bar. Within twenty-five miles of the open ocean, and with a perfectly straight and clear course out into deep water, the port is nevertheless so situated as to be completely landlocked and protected from storms at all seasons. The Elizabeth river, a tidal estuary setting in from the Chesapeake, affords a wide, calm, deep roadstead along the water front of Norfolk and of its sister city, Portsmouth with twenty-five feet of water at the docks, and ample opportunity for loading and unloading the largest vessels with the utmost ease and dispatch.

THE TERMINAL FACILITIES ARE EXCELLENT.

The railways run directly to the water's edge, and freight is transferred to vessels with the least possible labor and delay, without the assistance of draymen, lighters, or any other expensive means. Another advantage is the climate, which is so mild that outdoor as well as indoor work can be carried on without a day's interruption, all the year round; and still another is the abundance of cheap labor here available.

THE GEOGRAPHICAL POSITION

of Norfolk is extremely favorable to its commercial prosperity. A glance at the map will show that Norfolk is the natural outlet of the vast region comprising the greater portion of what is generally known as the New South.

Louisiana, Texas, southeastern Georgia, Florida and South Carolina may find it more convenient to export by way of New Orleans, Galveston, Savannah and Charleston, but the great coal, iron, tobacco, cotton, lumber, tar and food producing regions of Virginia, North Carolina, Tennessee, Kentucky, Alabama and upper Georgia naturally seek Norfolk as the nearest good seaport on the route from the southwest to the markets in New York, New England, New Jersey, Pennsylvania and Europe. Given adequate means of transportation, the route by way of Norfolk would afford the smallest possible railway mileage and the cheapest and best methods of communication between producers and consumers.

ITS TRANSPORTATION FACILITIES.

Norfolk now has nine railroads, and others are in contemplation. Six of the nine are important trunk lines, conveying here from the North, the West and the South, and most of them have been perfected during the last year or two. The imposing Norfolk and Western road, traversing the entire southern portion of Virginia, and rendering invaluable aid in the work of developing and marketing the rich ores of the Virginia and Tennessee mountains. The Seaboard and Roanoke runs down into North Carolina and makes important connections at Weldon, Raleigh, etc. The Atlantic and Danville is another trunk line running in the same general direction, and is intending to make far western connections in the near future. The Norfolk and Carolina is a new line tapping the Atlantic coast line in North Carolina, and built in the interests of that line and of the West Point Terminal, to secure for those corporations the advantage of a Norfolk terminus. The Chesapeake and Ohio, the rails of which reach tidewater at Newport News, has preferred to establish its official eastern terminus at Norfolk, and makes connections between those two points by a line of steamboats. Finally we have the direct and important connection with the metropolis, known as the New York, Philadelphia and Norfolk road, which does an immense business both in passenger traffic and in the transportation of truck, farm produce and sea food. Besides these there is the Norfolk and Southern, running to Edenton, N. C., on Albemarle Sound, a valuable ally of the truck farmers and oystermen of one of the most productive portions of the country. The five great lines leading to Norfolk from the west and southwest bring hither a heavy freight of cotton, coal and mineral ores, and other products of the interior.

RAILROADS ARE NOT BUILT FOR FUN,

and those who have invested millions of dollars in the construction of five competing lines to Norfolk may be presumed to know what they are about. They know, or at least they evidently believe, that Norfolk is destined to be a commercial centre of the first rank. They perceive the various natural advantages already named, and they look forward to the time when the bulk of the exports of the South will come to Norfolk for trans-shipment to Europe and to the North, and thus avoid the heavy expense of railway carriage to most Northern ports. In conformity with their views, the commerce of Norfolk, always noteworthy as to volume and value, is now seen to be advancing with steady and even rapid strides. The city has daily communication by steamer with Richmond, Washington and Baltimore, and almost daily with New York.

ITS INDUSTRIES.

Norfolk has one grain elevator, two cotton mills, and several machine shops, where locomotives, carriages, agricultural implements, etc., are made. The cheapness with which coal and iron can be now brought hither points to a rapid development of these industries. Another very important factor in the business activity of the city and vicinity is the truck farming industry. The finest truck farms in the United States are in the suburbs of Norfolk, and their savory products find their way regularly to New York, Philadelphia, and other great Northern markets within twenty-four or thirty-six hours after they are harvested. An analogous industry is the fish and oyster industry of Norfolk, which is very extensive, and is connected with the Northern markets in like manner.

Now, thanks to the improved transportation facilities, Norfolk is reaching out with her wonderful products to all parts of the country and to the world, and the end is not yet—in fact, it is the belief of the best informed authorities that the city is only at the beginning of a mighty prosperity.

ITS ATTRACTIONS.

The condition of the real estate market is usually a good index to the actual prosperity of a place. Real estate was cheap and slow a few years ago. The change that has taken place within three short years is almost miraculous. New life has entered the veins of the citizens. The population has increased nearly 60 per cent. since 1880, and now numbers about 40,000. The area of the city has been extended lately to more than treble its former size, taking in the suburban villages of Brambleton and Atlantic City. On the other side of the river Portsmouth and Berkley—practically a part of Norfolk—show similar advancement, and new settlements called South Norfolk and West Norfolk have been started. On the Bay and Ocean the beautiful new Summer Resorts, Ocean View and Virginia Beach, have contributed to the general pleasure and prosperity, and the lands lying alongside the railroads leading to those places are in process of rapid development. A large park on the river front, similar to the Battery Park in New York, has been ordered by the city and will soon be begun. Another park at the East End, involving many picturesque landscape features, is among the probabilities ; and still another, beyond the present city limits, is talked of. In the northern part of the city, between the old and new boundary lines, there will be, ere long, some

FINE ORNAMENTAL ADDITIONS

in the way of wide avenues and winding drives, bordered, eventually, doubtless, by handsome residences. In the present fashionable quarter of the city a large number of costly new houses in the most modern styles have been erected recently, and there is much activity in building this season in all parts of the town. The best streets, like Bute, Freemason, etc., are beautiful gardens and bowers, with a wealth of towering magnolias, luxuriant roses and all manner of lovely trees and flowers.

The city has been improved radically and incalculably during the last two years by the introduction of a thorough system of sewerage, followed by a re-paving of the principal streets. Previously there were no sewers at all and the pavement was of the poorest kind of cobblestone. Now twenty-two miles of sewers afford perfect drainage, and the cobble is rapidly giving place to the best kind of block pavement, which is to be laid, eventually, through the main body of the town.

THE WATER SUPPLY

Is ample and of excellent quality. The service has been recently reorganized in accordance with the most approved modern ideas. Two years ago the supply was only sufficient for 20,000 persons, at the outside, owing to defective service. The old apparatus caused a loss of more than 75 per cent. of the water power; but now, since the introduction of new machinery and larger pipes the supply is sufficient for 100,000 persons and the loss is not more than 10 per cent. For these great improvements Norfolk is, in a large measure, indebted to the enterprise and ability of its accomplished City Engineer, Mr. William T. Brooke, who has labored incessantly during the last eight years in behalf of the city's best interest. Other leading citizens and the city press deserve much credit also for their energetic efforts and public spirit.

ACTIVITY IN REAL ESTATE.

The effect of all these improvements on the value of real estate has been very striking. Three typical cases may be cited. In Brambleton three lots which were bought four years ago for $30 apiece were sold, the other day, for $900 apiece, and dozens of parallel transactions in that suburb might be mentioned. On Bute street a lot purchased three years ago for $1,500 has just been sold for $4,000. In the northern extension of the city a tract of fifty-five acres, which was considered almost valueless, and was exchanged for an old panorama, worth, perhaps, $500, a few years ago, was recently sold for $90,000, and is to be converted into building lots. These are fair illustrations of the recent rise in real estate in Norfolk. Outside capital is flowing in to take advantage of this activity. Half a dozen companies for the improvement of real estate and the institution and encouragement of manufacturers have been formed and are busily at work. These companies are composed of capitalists not only of Norfolk, but also of New York, Philadelphia and England, who have learned the facts detailed in this letter, and have acted accordingly. They know that Norfolk is the greatest lumber, fish and vegetable produce centre in the South; that it is the third cotton port in the country, and bids fair to become the second, if not the first; that it is

From the interior ; that its receipts of lumber last year were over 350,000,000 feet, of meat nearly 20,000,000 pounds, of coal more than 1,000,060,and that these figures show an increase of about 100 per cent. over those of 1888 ; that the population is rapidly increasing, the price of real estate advancing by leaps and bounds, and the modernization of the city nearing a complete accomplishment : that the climate is so balmy and the soil so fertile that two or three crops are raised annually with scarce any artificial fertilization ; and, finally, that the society of the town is in the highest degree refined and agreeable.

No wonder that strangers and outside capital are now attracted to Norfolk, and that her prosperity in these latter days is so much greater than its old citizens ever saw or even dreamed of in the times before the Merrimac steamed out of the Elizabeth river.

A NEW OUTLET FOR OHIO.

C. O. Hunter, Esq., of the law firm of Earnhart, Hunter & Butler, of Columbus, Ohio, wrote the following letter to the Evening *Dispatch*, of that city, his observations of this port, as an outlet for central Ohio, during a visit to Norfolk and Fortress Monroe, in June, 1890 :

FORTRESS MONROE, JUNE 27.—The absorption of the Scioto Valley Railway Company by the Norfolk and Western Railroad System is a fact of sufficient interest to the city of Columbus and central Ohio to at least lead to the inquiry of the possible benefits which may follow. That conservative Columbus, with her unexcelled natural advantages, her industrious spirit, her inexorable push and her financial strength may appreciate the opportunities which now lie at her threshold, a few facts by way of education may not here be amiss.

THE NORFOLK AND WESTERN RAILROAD

system, comprising more than 1,200 miles, is owned and officered by far-seeing, enterprising and active people. The railway is subsidiary, or the vehicle on which they carry to successful ends the numerous investments which they make in undeveloped lands, minerals, timbers, town cites, steam-boats and barge interests, terminal, wharf properties, warehouses, grain elevators, traffic facilities, etc. They arrange and manage so that each interest feeds, nourishes, supports and strengthens every other.

The original main line of 408 miles extends between Norfolk and Bristol, Tenn., and is now being double-tracked to accommodate the vast volume of lumber, coal, iron and cotton freights intended for export, coast and foreign. There are many branch lines, with others in progress of construction, and to be completed within the coming year. It connects by one branch of the road with lines that lead to Wilmington, N. C., and to the southwest; it is completing its Clinch Valley extension to a point in Wise county, Va., near the Kentucky line, and to connect with the Louisville and Nashville system, running from New Orleans to Chicago, and also from the New river southwestern coal fields division of the road northwestardly to the Ohio river, there by bridge to connect with the Scioto and Hocking Valleys, which are arteries into central Ohio, the very heart of the republic.

The liberal policy of its management has encouraged immigration and investment all along its line, and that most promising region of southwestern Virginia is now responding everywhere to the touch of capital and enterprise.

With the Scioto Valley thus absorbed and the Kanawa and Michigan by the Chesapeake and Ohio, two additional new rival and direct seaboard routes leading to the deepest and most

COMMODIOUS HARBOR OF THE WORLD.

So large, indeed, that the entire shipping of the globe could here find a haven, having, as she has, a double coast defense through her natural channel and byway of the Albemarle and Chesapeake canal, connecting Chesapeake Bay with Currituck, Albemarle, Pamlico, Cove and Bogue Sounds and their tributary streams.

Norfolk lies on the north bank of the Elizabeth river, at the confluence of the eastern and western branches of that stream, eight miles from Hampton Roads and twenty-three miles from Capes Charles and Henry, on the Atlantic coast. The channel of the river at the city is between 1,000 and 1,200 feet wide and twenty-two feet deep, low tide; the current is about one mile per hour.

The county of Norfolk has a population of about 100,000; upwards of 60,000 inhabitants residing within the limits of the port of customs, a territory comprising Norfolk proper, Brambleton and Berkley, suburbs and Portsmouth, which has a city government of its own.

For seventeen miles from Craney Island, five miles down from the two cities to a point twelve miles up stream from them, the channel averages one and a quarter miles in breadth, and with three feet of tide, twenty-five deep at low water and twenty-seven at the flood.

VESSELS OF TWENTY-SEVEN HUNDRED TONS

measurement can easily come up to the wharves of both Norfolk and Portsmouth, and those of six thousand tons, gross, have entered. As for Hampton Roads, the "Great Eastern," leviathan of ships as she was, found ample sea room in it.

More than one thousand deep water vessels enter this harbor every year, and perhaps one hundred and fifty carry foreign flags. Besides those of the port proper, a Liverpool and Brazilian mail line run from Newport News, eight miles from Norfolk, and in connection with the Chesapeake and Ohio railway.

The World's Fair bill, as passed Congress, provides that a naval review of the ships of this and other nations shall be held in the harbor of New York in April, 1893, and that for this purpose they shall rendezvous at Hampton Roads before proceeding to New York.

The cotton export exceeds that of New York. Last year about 500,000 bales were shipped. The products grown are exceedingly varied, the ground easily worked, and modern agriculture unknown. With development this country will become

THE BELGIUM OF AMERICA.

The feature of the agriculture found about Norfolk is the trucking or growing of vegetables for Northern markets. The soil is warm, the climate favorable, the rainfall plentiful. There are about 40,000 acres in this section devoted to trucking.

THE COUNTRY AROUND NORFOLK.

(From "Virginia as She Is," issued 1889, by the State Board of Agriculture.)

Norfolk County lies in the southeast corner of the State, bordering on Hampton Roads and Chesapeake Bay, with only one county, Princess Anne, between it and the sea. It is about thirty-two miles long, north and south, and seventeen miles wide, containing nearly 550 square miles. It is bounded on the north by Chesapeake Bay and Hampton Roads, on the east by Princess Anne County, on the south by North Carolina, and on the west by Nansemond County, Elizabeth River and Hampton Roads. The county is penetrated by several arms of the sea, viz: Tanner's Creek, Broad Creek, Mason's Creek and Deep Creek which, with the three branches of the Elizabeth River, viz: the "Eastern Branch," "Western Branch" and "Southern Branch," constitute a very *fine water system*, and places each farm in Norfolk County within three miles of water transportation. This insures to the Norfolk County farmer the cheapest transportation in the world. Two canals connect the waters of the Chesapeake with those of the North Carolina system of sounds and rivers, thus making all of eastern North Carolina tributary to Norfolk harbor by water. Nine railroads terminate in Norfolk harbor, cutting Norfolk County in all directions. *Nine beautiful shell turnpikes* also traverse Norfolk County from all points of the compass, centering on our fine harbor. Therefore, we may safely claim that the Norfolk County farmer is better supplied with transportation facilities than the farmers of any other county in the United States. All the streams of water in Norfolk County are effected by the tide, the tide ebbing and flowing to the very heads of all the streams. This constant ebbing and flowing of the tide carries the salt pure waters of the ocean twice each twenty-four hours up all these streams, and makes it quite impossible for any water to become stagnant or impure. These arms of the sea also afford the finest natural drainage known. The excess of rainfall running into them without ever doing a dollars worth of damage by flood or freshet. *The soil of Norfolk County* is of two general kinds, viz: a clay loam and a sandy loam, *all* underlaid with a good, substantial clay sub-soil. The surface of the county is from eight to twenty feet above the sea level. The mean annual rainfall is about fifty-two inches, well distributed throughout the year, of which amount about thirty-five inches falls during the growing season, say from the 1st of March to the 1st of October. The thermometer ranges in summer from 70° to 90°, seldom going to 95° above zero, while in winter it never goes below 20° above zero more than on three days, all told, during the winter. This cutting off of the two extremes of heat and cold is caused by the fact that the country is practically surrounded on three sides by salt water, and the water never goes to either extreme, as the water temperature is quite uniform throughout the year. *"The Gulf Stream,"* that great wonder of the Atlantic, which rolls only a few miles off our coast, on its way to Europe, has a very pleasing effect on our climate, especially on our winter climate. Norfolk County annually produces from $2,000,000 to $3,000,000 worth of market garden vegetables. *The famous Dismal Swamp* is on a hillside twenty-seven feet above the level of the sea in this harbor. If a wide and deep ditch were dug from tidewater to the lake in the centre of this Swamp the water thereof would run out to the sea like a mill race, and the Swamp would be a thing of the past. This Swamp was surveyed by Washington at an early day, and the famous Dismal Swamp Canal was surveyed and located by him, and he owned large tracts in the Swamp. There are no waters in the United States so pure as those of this Swamp. Government vessels leaving this harbor for long ocean voyages secure this juniper water from the Swamp on account of both its medicinal and keeping qualities. Invalids who, with rod and gun, go into this Swamp and spend a few weeks or months sleeping on juniper boughs, drinking juniper water and inhaling the juniper impregnated air rapidly improve in health, appetite and general robustness.

MASSACHUSETTS AND VIRGININA.

(From Norfolk Landmark, November 27, 1890.)

There are many Virginians so conservative that they bend over backwards to keep from leaning a little forward. Progress and growth to them mean extravagance and inflation. The brilliant prospects which are pictured for their state and for their own localities, as well as others, are to them the figments of a feverish dream. Nevertheless things move on and the doubt of to-day becomes the reality of to-morrow.

When the question is asked why should not Virginia do what other States with no greater natural resources and not so favorable a situation have done, there is no answer. No man can say, for there is no reason. On the contrary there is every reason why she should do what other States have done, and more. Every reason why her villages should rapidly grow into towns, her towns into cities and her cities into vast metropolitan proportions.

A writer in the New York *Journal of Commerce*, a conservative and unimaginative newspaper, discussed, the other day, in an article of some length, the comparative advantages of Massachusetts and Virginia in respect to development.

"What men have done," says he, "men can do again. What Massachusetts has done Virginia can do. The Bay State has only one advantage over us. Her cold east winds have carried the croaker to the only place cold enough and dark enough to make him feel at home. He is dead and buried. He croaks no more. So much for a bad climate. In all soberness and truth, Massachusetts is superior to Virginia only in the splendid energy and the daring business courage of her men. If any man knows of one gift with which nature has more richly endowed her than Virginia let him name it. Let us compare the two States. In climate the Old Dominion is to the Bay State as Paradise is to Purgatory. In the variety of her crops and the generosity of her soil, Virginia is unsurpassed; in harbors and in water power, in timber and in the variety of wealth of her mineral deposits, few, if any, States surpass her. Take all in all, the round world holds no fairer realm. Massachusetts has an area of 8,030 square miles. Virginia has five times as much territory, capable of supporting two men where Massachusetts supports one."

A VOICE FROM CAMBRIDGE.

By Edward Stack, Special Correspondent of the Cambridge, Mass., Tribune, October 13th, 1890.

THE CITY OF NORFOLK.

The heavy sales of real estate which have taken place in the city of Norfolk within the last few weeks are having the natural effect, and the movements of real estate are watched closely as well by outside parties as by the capitalists within the city.

When we consider the amount invested by outside parties in Virginia within the last seven years—that of Philadelphia alone being upwards of $7,000,000—the profitable development of her mineral mountains, the extension of the railroad interests of the state, the appreciation of properties, the enormous amount of cash paid to mechanics, miners and laboring men, and lastly, the great consumption of material for building purposes—considering all these facts, do the rise and progress of about twelve young cities show a result inconsistent with what might reasonably be expected?

My own opinion is that the advance apparent is a conservative result of the

MIGHTY INFLUENCES AT WORK,

and that the day is not far distant when a greater prosperity will show itself. When we cannot rule or foresee the order of events, then our wisest course is to set our sails to the breezes that blow and go on with the tide. There is a great deal of conservatism in Norfolk, but the city must accept the inevitable, and represent by its progress the destiny that awaits the State. Norfolk was always a lively city when compared with other large cities of Virginia. Its population to-day may be set down at from 35,000 to 40,000, while the immediate surroundings of Norfolk enable the city to draw benefits from a population of about 60,000. Portsmouth, with nearly 14,000 inhabitants, might well be under the same city government, and Berkley is but a suburb of Norfolk. The prosperity of the city to-day is unmistakable.

EVERY INTEREST IS ADVANCING,

and shows by figures a cheering ratio in excess of last year's computations.

Norfolk is deeply interested in the prosperity of Western Virginia, for all and any movement increasing the wealth of that portion of the State invigorates the business life of Norfolk. The coal of Pocahontas is borne to tide water at Norfolk, and hundreds of thousands of tons are shipped at the port. The cotton traffic alone brings to the city 3,000 bales a day, and the foreign cotton fleet keeps the compresses busy even to the working of the machinery day and night. The cotton men expect the receipts of the port to run up to 700,000 bales this season

FREEDOM FROM ICE

in the harbor, deep water and a good anchorage constitute the essentials which go to establish a great harbor or shipping port. All these essentials are possessed by Norfolk, and though her place to-day as a city is nothing in proportion to the importance she holds in her harbor, she can proudly look upon twenty-five lines of steamers departing each day from her port. In addition to these, her land transportation shows her to possess, with ten lines entering the city more railroads than Richmond.

Norfolk has entered upon

A GREAT CAREER OF PROSPERITY,

and it is not improbable that the city, under its influence, will grow to a population of 100,000 within seven years. All are of the opinion that Norfolk will be the largest city in the State; there has been no competitor for that position but Richmond, and a comparison of the progress in both cities leaves little doubt that the opinion pronounced will be fulfilled.

Gardening for market is carried on extensively all around Norfolk, and the value of the productions raised forms no small item in the exports. I have never seen a city of 100,000 a market as well supplied as I saw the Saturday I was in Norfolk. The farmers in this part of Virginia are prosperous. I have heard of one who made $20,000 in one year from 100 acres of land. Of course, this is an exception, but it shows what can be done. With such a port as that of Norfolk, by its nearness to the centers of population, north and eastward, there is no limit to the profitable expansion of such pursuits. Two crops are often taken from the same ground under the influence of the genial climate of Virginia.

THE YIELD OF FARM PRODUCTIONS

shipped from the port of Norfolk for 1890 will, it is estimated, reach the enormous amount of $4,500,000. These figures are enough to show the value of farming industries tributary to the city.

The surveys have been ordered and the work of construction will soon begin on a belt line of railroad to encircle Norfolk, Portsmouth and Berkley, connecting all the leading railroad lines, and furnishing facilities for transferring cars to and from these lines and to the various manufactories and wharves. This railway will bring all lines centering here into one union depot.

Norfolk offers unequalled advantages for the establishment of mechanical industries, both large and small. There are already a number here, including two cotton factories, with another in course of organization, the last with a capital of $300,000; shirt factories, basket factories, sash and blind factories, fertilizer factories on a large scale, shoe factories, plow works, iron foundries and agricultural implement factories, brick yards, a large carriage manufactory and extensive coffee roasting and peanut establishments. Negotiations are now being completed for a large steel plant, which will give employment to 5,000 hands.

MANUFACTURING ENTERPRISES

are to-day seeking for Southern locations, and Norfolk, as a site possessing great advantages, cannot be overlooked. The new industries which will be immediately instituted will be a car works, the Chesapeake Knitting Mills, a cotton factory and flouring mills, which are to cost over $1,000,000, and will insure employment to several hundred hands.

RAILWAY FACILITIES.

The building of two new and important railroads during the year goes to sustain the opinion so long held by many that Norfolk is destined to become the great centre of the Atlantic coast; but the advent of two new roads by no means embraces all the acquirements in this direction. The Norfolk and Western railroad has contracted for the extension of its line to the Ohio river, including a bridge across that great water highway, and has acquired 131 miles of additional track by the purchase of the Scioto Valley railroad, which penetrates the richest portion of the great state of Ohio, and at Columbus connects with railroads diverging to every point of the compass.

The value of this purchase to Norfolk is equal to the securing of an independent line, and her interest in the Shenandoah Valley road is of great consequence also. With this may be mentioned the extension of the Seaboard Air Line to Atlanta, and the chartering of several new roads, among them the Virginia, Missouri and Pacific, which is the proposed air line between Norfolk and the Golden Gate.

By a special act of Congress Hampton Roads has been designated as

THE NAVAL RENDEZVOUS OF THE WORLD

on the occasion of the World's Fair at Chicago, which means that all the navies of the world will be represented there. The meeting of those ships will be one of the grand historical events of the world, and preparations are being made commensurate with its dignity.

DELIGHTFUL SURROUNDINGS.

There is not, perhaps, a city in America that can boast of more delightful surroundings than Norfolk. The points of interest and of beauty around the harbor have established its fame as a summer and winter resort. The breezes from the open sea provide a refreshing coolness from the summer heat, and the temperate mildness of Virginia offers a retreat from the freezing condition of a Northern climate. Norfolk will be a city of 100,000 people in seven years.

Ships for the United States Navy are being built at Norfolk, and it can boast of

THE FINEST DRY DOCK,

not excepting California, in the United States. The steamers City of Paris and Teutonic, the greyhounds of the Atlantic, use Pocahontas coal, which is shipped from the port of Norfolk. The scenes of the battle between the Merrimac and Monitor, which was fought in Hampton Roads, is almost within sight of the city, and is pointed out as you are borne in magnificent steamers to points of interest in the harbor. For a charge of fifty cents a beautiful steamer will convey you from the city to Fortress Monroe, whose bristling cannons protect the entrance to the harbor. Close to the Fort is the Hygeia Hotel, the grandest institution of the kind in the world. The harbor of Norfolk could afford shelter to all the shipping of the world, and place at their disposal twenty-eight feet of water at low tide.

In this review of this interesting city many items of interest and of public worth are left unnoticed and undescribed. The city is lighted by electricity and gas; schools and churches are so situated as to show that religion and education go hand in hand for the general good. The street car system is found to be insufficient for the new growth of the city, and more than one company to construct an electric car system has been incorporated. The future will see in this country a great ship building boom, and Norfolk will certainly take a lead as a ship building port. There are being completed here now large steel cruisers for the Navy.

A BELT LINE AROUND THE CITY.

From the Cornucopia.

It is generally well known that the facilities enjoyed by this seaport (Norfolk) for the quick and cheap transferring and handling of all kinds of freight are simply unrivalled in the United States. There is no other seaport in the Union where the ocean steamers and the many lines of rail are so closely and advantageously connected as here. Notwithstanding this a move is now on foot to add very materially to these advantages. This move is the "Belt Line," so called because it will "belt" or girdle the cities of Portsmouth, Berkley and Norfolk, and closely connect five of the great lines of rail terminating on deep water in this grand harbor. This "Belt Line" will closely connect and secure harmonious and pleasant traffic relations between the following railroads, viz: The "Norfolk and Western," "Norfolk and Carolina," Norfolk and Southern," "Seaboard and Roanoke," and "Atlantic and Danville." As soon as the Virginia Beach Railroad is changed from a narrow to standard guage it will then include that line, making six lines of rail to be benefitted by this "Belt Line." The first two named roads are the ones actively engaged in pushing this splendid enterprise. As stated above, it is to belt the cities on this harbor with a line of steel just outside the present limits of these cities. It opens up a fine stretch of country and brings into market some fine bodies of land situated admirably for all kind of manufacturing purposes, as well as for additions to the cities above named. The finest sites for factories can be secured on this "Belt Line." As a factory located on the "Belt Line" is practically located on *all* the above named six lines of road connected by the said "Belt Line."

At this time there is no section in the United States that offers such advantages to the manufacturers as Norfolk, Va. The raw material can be brought to the factory by any one of the numerous steamboat or railroad lines entering here, while the manufactured articles can be shipped to all points of the compass at the most favorable rates known. The freight service is fine and the rates very low indeed. The "Belt Line" is a good move in the right direction.

PREDICTIONS.

From the Cornucopia.

In less than ten years time the Government will have extensive and expensive fortifications at Cape Henry—one of the guardian capes of the royal Chesapeake. A railroad will be built from Norfolk either direct to Cape Henry or via Ocean View and thence along the shores of the Chesapeake. The old canal project, of connecting the waters of the Eastern Branch of the Elizabeth River with those of Lynnhaven will be revived and carried out. A rolling mill will be established at Lambert's Point. The whole coast from Sewall's Point around to Currituck inlet will be one continuous health and pleasure resort, both in summer and winter. Every foot of land with a fair water frontage will double twice or more in value. Norfolk will extend from Tanner's Creek on the north to Broad Creek on the east. West Norfolk will extend across to the Nansemond River, and Portsmouth will be offering town lots in the great Dismal Swamp, offering as inducements canal transportation and juniper water. The Belt Line will girdle the "Twin Cities." Electricity will propel our street cars. The air line railroad from Charleston, S. C., to Norfolk, will be built. The Norfolk and Western railroad will be double-tracked its entire length. The Chesapeake and Ohio will have a deep sea terminus on the south end of Chesapeake Bay.

UP TO DATE—JANUARY, 1891.

Since the action of the Chamber of Commerce late in October last, to print 10,000 copies of this report, pains have been taken to elaborate and expand the information then given, and include transactions which have been occurring daily since that time. In fact, it was deemed advisable to extend the report up to the close of the year 1890, and this resolve now enables us to make some of our figures more interesting to those who are seizing with avidity every line appertaining to Norfolk. Transactions in trade, commerce, real estate, finances, etc., are now given as thoroughly as can be had on the eve of 1891, and comparison made when possible.

Elsewhere we give the transfers of real estate in Norfolk, Portsmouth and the county of Norfolk, and any comparison of figures with former years in this branch of business would be like comparing a mountain to a mole hill, or John L. Sullivan to Tom Thumb. This remarkable activity has been elsewhere accounted for, and from present indications is likely to continue around Norfolk for some time to come.

The conditions here are so well marked, and understood, that present values are more likely to advance than recede. Yet, if this opinion proves erroneous, time will show that those who have builded well will fare well in the end.

THE RECEIPTS OF COTTON at this port for the four months ending December 31st, 1890, show 405,781 bales, against 301,572 bales for same period ending December 31, 1889, showing an increase of 104,209 bales. These periodical reports of Mr. Bell, the Secretary and Superintendent of the Cotton Exchange, are very interesting reading to those who are watching with keen interest the trade of this port

IN GENERAL MERCHANDISE the year 1890 shows in many articles large gains over the preceding year.

Receipts of lumber and logs for

1890	359,509,693 feet.
1889	309,098,594 "
Increase	50,411,099 feet.

or more than fifty millions of feet increase over 1889.

Staves show some decline in the year past, but shingles held their own and reached fifty-three millions. Railroad ties show an increase of over a million. In grain, groceries and provisions the receipts show for the year in many articles a marked increase over the figures given herein for 1889 on pages 14 and 15. Coal oil reached 45,019 barrels, and cotton seed oil 53,213 barrels. Naval stores 43,058 barrels against 22,375 in 1889. Pocahontas coal increased for the year 140,000 bushels, or a total of 1,159,019 bushels for 1890.

The cotton crop in the Carolinas and eastern Virginia, as in the South generally, was a large one, and our receipts, elsewhere given, for the four months, September 1st to December 31st, have largely augmented our bank balances and exports.

Altogether our merchants have reason to rejoice over the results of the year; they find very few of their number missing from the ranks, and notwithstanding the financial cramp, which has been serious in many quarters, the trade and resources of the South have developed wonderful strength.

OUR BANKS AND CLEARING HOUSE.

From published reports made late in December, 1890, we condense the following figures :

CLEARING HOUSE FIGURES COMPARED FOR SIX YEARS.

1885	$33,228,851
1886	40,342,389
1887	42,013,162
1888	45,447,259
*1889	39,945,470
1890	48,210,486

*Accounted for by short cotton crop.

BANKING HOUSES.

	CAPITAL.
Norfolk National Bank	$400,000
Citizens' Bank	200.000
Marine Bank	100,000
Bank of Commerce	100.000
Norfolk Savings Bank	25,000
Norfolk Trust Company	20.000
Union Savings Bank	20,000
Merchants' and Mechanics' Savings Bank	10,000

Burruss, Son & Co. } Private Banks.
John D. Gordon & Co. }

Following figures embrace a condensed statement of the financial condition, in the aggregate, of the banking houses only :

Capital stock	$ 885,000
Surplus fund	160,000
Undivided profits	232,644
Deposits	4,080,867
Loans and discounts	3,447,802
Investments (bonds)	898,640

ENTERPRISES ESTABLISHED IN 1890.

There were completed, within the city limits, during the year 1890, the following enterprises :

One soap factory, of large capacity.

One four story warehouse, the largest in the State, for cleaning and preparing peanuts for the trade.

One boot and shoe factory.

One wagon and carriage factory.

One cotton and knitting factory.

One large, modern constructed hotel, on the main thoroughfare.

One flour mill, with the latest improvements and roller process.

There is in contemplation, with almost certain accomplishment during 1891, the following additional enterprises:

An ice factory, capacity sixty tons per day.

A cotton factory.

A packing house.

Chemical works.

Cotton seed oil mill.

Cotton yarn mill.

Paper and wooden box factory.

A hat factory, with the capacity for 400 operatives, removed here from New York.

To reach the several villages which are springing up within three miles of the city there will be horse and electric railway lines in all directions.

The purchasers of contiguous lands are pushing with wonderful energy the development of their properties, and the outlook for employment is very pleasing.

PORT CHARGES IN NORFOLK.

The following rates, now in force, are given for the use of those interested.

PILOTAGE FROM SEA TO NORFOLK.—Ten feet and under, $2.50 per foot; 13 feet and over 10, $3.00 per foot; 14 feet, $3.50 per foot; 16 feet, $4.00 per foot, and over 16 feet $4.50 per foot. The pilotage from Norfolk to the sea is at same rates.

Pilotage between Norfolk and Newport News, and in Norfolk harbor, $10.

Pilotage between Norfolk and West Point, $25.

WHARFAGE.—One cent, per net registered ton per day on steamers; on sailing vessels, one cent per ton per day on the first 300 tons register, and a half of one cent per ton per day on tonnage exceeding 300 tons.

Stevedoring cotton, 35 cents per bale; stevedoring dead weight, oak plank, 40 cents per ton; grain (bulk), $3.00 per 1,000 bushels.

TOWING—Shifting with ship's steam, $15.00; shifting without ship's steam, $25.00 to $30 00; harbor towage, $15.00.

Coal, $3.35 per long ton trimmed in bunkers.

WATER—Small quantities, ½c per gallon; large quantities, ¼c per gallon.

HARBOR MASTER—Fees (port), $5.00; docking fees, $5.00.

Quarantine fees, $7.00

The distance from Norfolk to British and Continental ports is the same as from New York, and shorter to South American ports.

Our proximity to the consuming marts of this country is shown by the following figures:

Boston, 20 hours by rail, 40 by water.

New York, 12 hours by rail, 21 by water.

Philadelphia, 10 hours by rail, 18 by water.

Baltimore, 8 hours by rail, 12 by water.

Washington, 7 hours by rail, 12 by water.

Richmond (State Capitol), by rail, 2½ hours, by the James river line, which has special historic attractions, 10 hours.

Cincinnati, by rail 23 hours.

Chicago, by rail 34 hours.

St. Louis, by rail 34 hours.

Norfolk is nearer than New York to San Francisco.

The Equitable Life Assurance Society

OF THE UNITED STATES.

THE LARGEST, STRONGEST & BEST LIFE ASSURANCE COMPANY IN THE WORLD.

Before Insuring your Life, call upon, or address

A. MYERS,

MANAGER AND GENERAL AGENT FOR EASTERN VA.,

61 Commerce Steeet, Norfolk, Va.

H. L. MYERS,

Local and Special Agent.

A. MYERS,
President Norfolk Real Estate Exchange.

H. L. MYERS.

A. MYERS & CO.,

Real Estate Agents and Auctioneers

No. 61 COMMERCE STREET,

NORFOLK, VA.

PROPERTY SOLD PRIVATELY OR AT AUCTION.

Houses and Lots in all parts of Norfolk and surrounding country for sale.

Farms for sale.

TOWN OF LAMBERT'S POINT

ADJOINING THE CITY OF NORFOLK.

SITUATION.

The large reservation of the Norfolk and Western Railroad adjoins the northwest boundary of the city of Norfolk, lying about two miles from the City Hall. Immediately North of this grand railroad terminus, the Lambert's Point Company, and the Lambert's Point Land Company, have purchased one hundred and sixty-five acres of high and well-drained land, situated on the Elizabeth River; and have laid out in rectangular blocks the most beautiful and attractive town site in Eastern Virginia. As soon as the population justifies, an Electric Plant, Gas and Water Works will be established, supplying the two great necessities of domestic economy at a minimum cost. The town is now connected with the business part of Norfolk and Portsmouth by a steam ferry, and a street railway is to be constructed from the terminus of the city railway to the town of Lambert's Point as soon as possible. Pocahontas Avenue, 80 feet wide, extends from the Bowden's Ferry Road through the town and through a portion of the yard of the Norfolk and Western Railroad to the Elizabeth River. The lots are 25x125 feet, and afford unrivalled sites for suburban residences. Lambert's Point Road, 60 feet wide, divides the town from the railroad reservation. Shenandoah, Rappahannock and Potomac Streets, 60 feet wide, with lots 25x125 feet and 25x100 feet, afford opportunities for mechanics, clerks and artisans employed by the Railroad Company, in its offices, warehouses and shops, and by other large industries to be erected within the limits of the town, to secure pleasant and convenient homes at moderate prices. The Ocean Terminus of the Norfolk and Western System will make Lambert's Point within two years the busiest commercial centre in the southern states, and will alone give employment to enough inhabitants to make every lot in the new town of great intrinsic value, independent of the other industries which are contemplated by the two companies in their manufacturing reservations.

COAL.

There is now shipped from the Lambert's Point Coal Pier nearly 100,000 tons of Pocahontas Coal per month, and within the year ending December 31st, 1890, 384 foreign steamships have called at this pier for coals. Another immense coal pier constructed of iron is fast nearing completion, and it is expected that one million and a half tons of Pocahontas steam coal will be shipped from Lambert's Point this year. Besides the Pocahontas coal, shipment of gas coal from the Clinch Valley to Lambert's Point has commenced; and it is estimated that a quarter of a million of tons of this superior gas coal will be received for shipment this year. Steam and gas coal are available at minimum tidewater prices at the town of Lambert's Point.

IRON.

Preparations are being made to ship a large portion of the product of the iron furnaces tributary to the Norfolk and Western System, to Lambert's Point, and to have a large storage yard for the pig iron and iron ore, where it can be held, negotiable receipts being issued for the same. Manufacturers in the town of Lambert's Point can obtain the ore and pig iron at lowest coastwise prices.

STOCK YARDS.

A company is being formed to erect extensive stock yards for the shipment of cattle, adjoining the Norfolk and Western reservation on the east and convenient to the town of Lambert's Point; but sufficiently distant to prevent its being objectionable.

COTTON DISTRICT.

It is contemplated to dedicate twenty acres more or less of the Railroad reservation at Lambert's Point, with piers, fireproof warehouses, presses, sheds, etc., for handling all the cotton business of the port of Norfolk and Portsmouth in the most approved manner at a minimum cost.

THROUGH COASTWISE AND FOREIGN BUSINESS.

The Norfolk and Western Railroad Company has filled in some thirty acres of its water front, and constructed the largest merchandise warehouse in the South for accommodating its coastwise and foreign business, with ample room for, erecting additional warehouses as business demands. These wharves, like those of the coal piers, can accommodate the largest steamships afloat, having 26 feet of water at low tide.

COMPLETION OF THE CLINCH VALLEY AND OHIO EXTENSIONS.

With the completion of the Clinch Valley extension to connect with the vast Louisville and Nashville System, in 1891, and the Ohio extension to connect with the Scioto Valley Railroad to Columbus, Ohio, in 1892, there will pour into Lambert's Point a vast amount of cotton, grain, tobacco, provisions, etc., from the Northwest, West and Southwest, and make the mile of piers at Lambert's Point a busy hive of industry, sufficient to support a large community, which will need homes in the town of Lambert's Point.

THE MACHINE SHOPS OF THE EASTERN DIVISION.

The machine shops of the Eastern Division of this great railroad system will be situated on the street which separates the Railroad property from the town of Lambert's Point, and will steadily employ from 250 to 300 skilled machinists. The repairs of the coal cars, which are emptied here, will alone give employment to a large force of mechanics.

THE TERMINUS OF THE BELT LINE.

The deep water terminus of the Belt Line, which will shortly be commenced to connect all the Railroad Systems coming to this harbor, will be at Lambert's Point; and manufacturers in the town of Lambert's Point will be enabled to receive Through Bills of Lading from any of the roads, so as to ship to any part of the continent by rail, while enjoying the facility of water carriage to all parts of the globe.

INDUSTRIES CONTEMPLATED.

The two Companies owning this property are negotiating for the establishment of a large Iron Ship Building Plant, Tin Plate Works, a Canning Establishment, a Lumber Mill, &c. Any Manufacturers looking for a site, having unsurpassed facilities for distribution by land and water would do well to correspond with the undersigned.

WATER SUPPLY.

An Artesian well has been planted at Lambert's Point, yielding, at six hundred feet, fifty gallons of good water per minute. The supply of water in the town of Lambert's Point may therefore be regarded as unlimited.

THE FIRST SUBURBAN PARK FOR NORFOLK CITY.

The beautiful park which these two Companies have dedicated forever to the public, and which every lot owner will have a right to enter and enjoy, is the first suburban park established in the neighborhood of Norfolk City, and when connected by a street railway with the city will be a great pleasure resort and add to the attractions of the town of Lambert's Point.

WILLIAM LAMB,

President Lambert's Point Co.,

and Lambert's Point Land Co.

FOR PURCHASE OF LOTS

Apply to the Members of the Norfolk City Real Estate Exchange.

BARTON MYERS.   F. M. KILLAM.

MYERS & Co.,

(ESTABLISHED 1586.)

REAL ESTATE,

NORFOLK, VA.

—AGENTS FOR—

NORFOLK WATER FRONT DEVELOPMENT CO.,
LAMBERT'S POINT COMPANY OF NORFOLK,
LAMBERT'S POINT WATER FRONT CO.
NEW NORFOLK LAND CO.,
NORFOLK LAND & IMPROVEMENT CO.,
LAMBERT'S POINT INVESTMENT CO.,
ATLANTIC IMPROVEMENT CO.,
WEST END REAL ESTATE CO.,
WEST ATLANTIC CITY LAND CO.,
NORFOLK ROLLISTON COMPANY.

CORRESPONDENCE SOLICITED.

Information and statistics furnished with regard to investments in Norfolk Real Estate and Stocks, and
investments made on orders from
outside parties.

HEADQUARTERS

—FOR—

NORTH CAROLINA PINE.

THE TUNIS LUMBER CO.,

NORFOLK, VA.

BAND AND GANG-SAWED LUMBER.

The Largest and Best Equipped Establishment in the
South, and in fact the Largest in America
in the same line of business.

Total output of their mills in 1890 was eighty millions of feet of
manufactured lumber.

The Company own stumpage enough to last many years, and
will, no doubt, continue at the head of the list in manufacturing
North Carolina Pine.

Facilities for shipping are unexcelled, both by rail and water.

Lumber delivered anywhere.

Write for particulars to NORFOLK., VA, or

No. 6 South Street, Baltimore, Md.

GO TO VIRGINIA !

WHERE THE DEVELOPMENT IS THE WIDEST !
WHERE THE OPPORTUNITIES ARE THE GREATEST !
WHERE ALL ARE WELCOME !

The most desirable location in the South for the manufacture of wagons, stoves, agricultural implements, furniture, or for foundries, machine shops, rolling mills, muck bar mills, tin plate works, cotton tie works, iron pipe works, car works, horse and mule shoe factories, nail works, glass works, cotton or woolen mills, tanneries, and diversified manufactures of every character are to be found in Virginia, along the line of the Norfolk & Western Railroad from Norfolk, Va., and Hagerstown, Md., to Bristol, Tenn., and upon its branch lines. Hard wood of every variety; pig iron from the furnaces at Lynchburg (2), Roanoke (3), Shenandoah (1), Pulaski (1 in operation and 1 under construction), Ivanhoe (1), Radford (1 now under construction), Salem, Graham, Max Meadows, Bristol and Buena Vista (1 at each point under construction); bar iron from the rolling mills at Richmond (1), Roanoke (1 in operation and 1 under construction), Lynchburg (1), Richlands and Shenandoah (1 now under construton at each point); coke and semi-bituminous coal from the Pocahontas Flat Top field; superior gas coals from the mines on the Clinch valley extension; glass sand from Tazewell county; cotton from the markets of the Southern States, and wool from the Western and Southern States and Territories, at advantageous freight rates. Favorable freight rates made upon raw materials to all factories established upon its lines, as well as to all points in the United States and Territories upon the manufactured articles.

Those seeking new fields for manufacturing establishments should not fail to investigate the wonderful development of iron, coal and coke industries that has been made within the past five years along the line of the Norfolk and Western Railroad, and the advantages offered by the State of Virginia in the supply of raw materials; by the Norfolk and Western Railroad in the matter of freight facilities and rates upon raw materials, and for reaching home, far-distant and foreign markets, and by the cities and towns along its lines in the way of advantageous sites, free or at moderate cost. Many of the cities and towns exempt manufacturing establishments from taxation for a series of years.

For further information as to freight and passenger rates and sources of supply of raw material, maps of the Norfolk and Western Railroad and its extensions now under construction, time-tables, pamphlet and reference book descriptive of the territory tributary to its lines, apply to

W. B. BEVILL,   **A. POPE,**
Gen'l Pass. Agt., Roanoke, Va.   Gen'l Frt. Agt., Roanoke, Va

CHAS. G. EDDY,
Vice-President, Roanoke, Va.

LIST OF MEMBERS—JANUARY, 1891.

Agelasto, A. M.,	(Ralli Bros.) Cotton buyers.
Allyn, Jos. T.,	Attorney-at-Law.
Allen, W. F. & Co.,	Wholesale grocers.
Barnard, W. H. & Co.,	Stoves, tinware, etc.
Bank of Commerce.,	T. A. Williams, pres.
Barber & Co.,	Agents for Liv. and London S. S. Lines.
Barrett, G. & R.,	Wholesale grocers.
Blackburn, J. B. & Co.,	Merchandise brokers.
Bruce & Terry.,	Wholesale grocers.
Borum, Jas. T.,	(Pearce & Borum) Cotton factors.
Burk & Co,	Clothiers and men's furnishings.
Burroughs & Bro.,	Attorneys-at-Law.
Burruss, Son & Co.,	Bankers.
Bowden, Geo. E.,	M. C.
Cassell & Cassell,	Architects.
Carney, S. B.,	Real estate.
Cooke, W. M. & Co.,	Grain dealers.
Cooke, Clark & Co.,	Sash, doors and blinds.
Cooke, R. B.,	Gen. F. and P. Agt. N. Y., P. & N. R.R.
Culpeper & Turner.,	Agents Old Dominion S. S. Co.
Davis, M. L. T. & Co.,	Wholesale grocers.
Day, John H. & Co.,	Produce commission.
Dillard, G. M.,	Attorney-at-Law.
Dobie, R. A. & Co.,	Cotton factors and general commission.
Doyle, W. H.,	Cashier Citizens' Bank.
Dodson, R. A.,	Manager New Atlantic Hotel.
Dunn, Geo. R.,	Real estate.
Edwards & Fiveash.,	Publishers *Public Ledger*.
Edwards, O. E.,	Pres. Virginia Pilot Association.
Elliott, Ghas. G.,	Treasurer Norfolk and Carolina R. R.
Everett Bros. & Gibson.,	Cotton factors.
Farquharson, D. H.,	Manager Baltimore United Oil Co.
Farmers Mfg. Co.,	J. Frank East, president.
Franklin, W. S.,	Auditor Va. and Tenn. Air Line.
Foster, W. E. & Co.,	Gas fitters and plumbers.
Gatling, N. P. & Co.,	Printers and stationers.
Graves, W. A.,	Retired ship builder.
Glennan, M.,	Publisher Norfolk *Virginian*.

Greenwood & Bro.,	Jewelers.
Grandy, C. W. & Son,	Cotton factors.
Groner, V. D.,	President Consolidated Compress Co's.
Gurley & Rogers,	Shingles and lumber.
Hamburger Bros.,	Wholesale tobacconists.
Harmanson & Heath.	Attorneys-at-Law.
Hodges, Harry,	President Etna Iron Works.
Howard, Paul R.,	Wood and willow ware, etc.
Hunter, J. W. & Co.,	Wholesale dry goods and notions.
Hudgins, H. C.	Gen. Pass. Agt. Norfolk Southern R. R.
Hill, Rowland,	Real estate.
Imp'ing and Ex'ing Salt Co.,	W. D. Denby, manager.
Johnson & Kilby,	Merchandise Brokers.
Jones, Jesse & Son,	Grain dealers.
Jordan, C. D..	Produce commission.
Johnson, G., Lumber Co.,	Lumber millers.
Johnston, Geo. W.,	Capitalist.
Lamb, Wm. & Co.,	Coal and shipping.
Landmark Co.,	Publishers *Landmark*.
Leigh, Bros. & Phelps.,	Real estate agents. (See ad.)
Lowenberg, David,	Capitalist.
Mayer & Co.,	Engineers' and machinists' supplies.
Mason, M. W. & Co.,	Real estate agents.
Myers & Co.,	Real estate. (See ad.)
Myers, A.,	Life insurance and real estate (see ad).
McCarrick, J. W.,	General agent Clyde Line.
McIntyre, F. P.,	Furniture, carpets, etc.
McIntosh, George,	Attorney-at-Law.
Nash, C. A. & Co..	Sash, doors and blinds.
Nottingham & Wrenn,	Ice, coal and wood.
N. and P. Transfer Co.,	Baggage agents.
Osborne, N. M.,	General agent N. & W. R. R.
Old Dom'ion Creosoting Co.,	Samuel D. Puller, manager. (See ad.)
Perry, J. W. & Co.,	Cotton factors.
Pollard, B. G. & Co.,	Cotton and general commission.
Poindexter, Parke L.,	Real estate agent.
Ramsey, C. G.,	President Norfolk National Bank.
Randall, Wm.	Agent Baltimore Steam Packet Co.

Reid, Chas & Son,	Fertilizers and staves.
Reynolds Bros.,	Cotton buyers and shipping.
Richardson, F.,	Insurance and real estate.
Roper, John L.,	President Roper Lumber Co.
Ruffin & Tomlin,	Attorneys-at-Law.
Smith & Pannill,	Real estate agents. (See ad.)
Smith, Peter & Co.,	Dry goods.
Smith, O. V.,	Agent Seaboard and Roanoke R. R.
Shields, L. H.,	Real estate.
Spandour, A. L.,	Artesian wells.
Stires, R. W.,	Truckers' package supplies.
Shoemaker, S. B.,	Gen. F. and P. Agt. N. & V. B. R. R.
Taylor, W. H.,	President Marine Bank.
Taylor, Washington & Co.,	Wholesale grocers.
Taylor & Loyall,	Fine groceries and liquors.
Taylor, G. W. & Co.,	Ice, coal and wood.
Taylor, S. J.,	Wines and liquors.
Thomas, S. J. & Co.,	Boot and shoe dealers.
Tredwell, A. & Co.,	Cotton factors.
Tunstall & Thom,	Attorneys-at-Law.
Tunis Lumber Co.,	North Carolina pine. (See ad.)
Tunis & Eccles,	Lumber dealers.
Umstadter, M. & Co.,	Dry goods and furniture.
Vance, E.,	Wines and liquors.
Vaughan & Barnes,	Cotton factors.
Vermillion, John,	Fine wines, liquors and segars.
Walke & Williams,	Drugs, paints, oils, etc.
Walke & Son,	General insurance agents.
Walke, Henry,	Hardware, steamboat and mill supplies.
Watters & Martin,	Wholesale hardware.
Weld, Franklin,	President A. & C. Canal Co.
Williams, T. A. & Co.,	Wholesale grocers.
Williams, H. C.,	Brick manufacturer.
White & Garnett,	Attorneys-at-Law.
White, J. B.,	Produce commission.
White, E. V. & Co.,	Railroad and steamboat supplies.
Womble, J. G. & Son,	Hardware dealers.
Wortley, R. M. Stuart,	President A. & D. R. R.
Wrenn, Whitehurst & Co.,	Agricultural implement manufacturers.
Wright, Richard H.,	Agent Merch. and Miners Trans. Co.
Zachary, R. Y.,	Merchandise broker.

On page 46, six lines up from bottom, read TONS instead of bushels of POCA-HONTAS COAL.

www.ingramcontent.com/pod-product-compliance
Lightning Source LLC
Chambersburg PA
CBHW021634270326
41931CB00008B/1017